THE COMPLETE GUIDE TO THE MUSIC OF

Edited by Robert Dimery
Cover & Book designed by Hilite Design & Reprographics Limited
Picture research by Nikki Russell

ISBN: 0.7119.6913.2
Order No: OP48075

Exclusive Distributors:
Book Sales Limited, 8/9 Frith Street, London W1V 5TZ, UK.
Music Sales Corporation, 257 Park Avenue South, New York, NY 10010, USA.
Music Sales Pty Limited, 120 Rothschild Avenue, Rosebery, NSW 2018, Australia.

To the Music Trade only:
Music Sales Limited, 8/9, Frith Street, London W1V 5TZ, UK.

Photo credits: Front and back cover Retna. All other pictures supplied by LFI.

Every effort has been made to trace the copyright holders of the photographs in this book but one or two were unreachable. We would be grateful if the photographers concerned would contact us.

Printed in Great Britain by Printwise (Haverhill) Limited, Suffolk

A catalogue record for this book is available from the British Library.

Visit Omnibus Press at http://www.omnibuspress.com

CONTENTS

Introduction

The music of Frank Zappa is above all a provocation, a smack in the face for public taste. Play one of his records, and you get an argument. His critics are legion, but then so are his fans. This guide doesn't pretend to be unpartisan. For this writer, Zappa was second only to Hendrix as a rock guitarist – and as composer, producer, bandleader and interviewee, second to no-one in rock at all thank you.

Luckily for us – now that he's gone – Zappa spent most of his time on this planet down in his basement studio constructing those weird little artefacts called 'albums': cunning collations of sounds, words and visuals. His records were so detailed and crafted and packed that Zappologists around the globe are still unravelling them – but here they are, all present and correct, in a complete guide.

Towards the end of his life, Zappa was asked by *Simpsons*' creator Matt Groening to expound on the concept of time. 'I think that everything is happening all the time,' he replied, 'and that the only reason why we think of time linearly is because we are conditioned to do it. That's because the human idea of stuff is: it has a beginning and an end. I don't think that's necessarily true. I think of time as a constant, a spherical constant...'. Zappa was delighted to find this idea in Stephen Hawking's *A Brief History Of Time* (this explains the dedication to Hawking in *The Real Frank Zappa Book*). Mystical? Bizarre? The weird thing is that the more you listen, the truer Zappa's words become. In what he called his oeuvre, everything really does seem to happen all the time!

When Frank Zappa died, journalists had to come up with snap synopses. The usual one ran: 'Sixties rock guitarist/scatologist who matured to become a classical composer and media spokesman'. This ignored the fact that Zappa composed scores before he even touched the guitar, and that everything he ever said or did –

even when conducting symphony orchestras – had a satirical, media-bucking edge. When he unveiled something "new", you could be sure that it was something he'd been thinking about for years, maybe forever; and that the indignation it would provoke was pre-echoed in advance, too.

In 1984 he released a triple-LP boxed-set named *Thing-Fish*, the soundtrack of a 'comedy musical'. Sack-cloth (or 'burlap') was reproduced all over box and booklet. In 1969 Zappa had told *Zig Zag* magazine about a musical called 'Captain Beefheart Versus The Grunt People'; the Grunt People, he explained, 'wear these clothes which are like burlap bags with fish and garbage sewn on them'. Did it ever dawn on the upstanding critics who condemned the 'vulgarity' of 'Titties & Beer' that its plot was actually a rewrite of 'A Soldier's Tale' by revered classical composer Igor Stravinsky? In the mid-80s, Zappa 'parodied' The Channels' 1956 doo-wop number 'The Closer You Are'; did his teen metal audience know that that he'd once released a whole album of this stuff (*Cruising With Ruben & the Jets*, 1969)? That in 1963 he'd written and recorded a song – 'Memories Of El Monte' – for doo-wop survivors The Penguins?

Like Mandelbrot's fractals, every Zappa grotesquery springs from some tiny detail in previous work (the celebrated sex yarn 'Dinah-Moe Humm' was heralded by a phrase in the sci-fi story inside the booklet that accompanied *Uncle Meat*). Zappa's cleverest trick – and one which still provokes frenzied speculation among Zappologists – was his ability to parody trends and music-biz absurdities before they appeared! Perhaps time is indeed an illusion...

Tracking Zappa's references and details can turn apparently sane individuals into gibbering loons (hello Danny, hello Gamma), visionaries who scream with delight at any mention of poodles or dental floss (or fat floating sofas). However, it can be said in their defence that this madness is worth the trip because Zappa's music is so wonderful:

riven with deliriously beautiful tunes, non-standard, bracing rhythms and succulent, east-of-Vienna harmonies. Most music – most culture – is judged these days according to a list of "politically correct" precepts that are both prim and prissy. Zappa blows the PC moralist sky-high, offering his listeners lurid aesthetic experience instead. If the response is 'I'm hip but of course I am offended' (as Zappa once characterised it), so much the worse for conventional mores and its blocked ears!

Despite his concept of time as a 'spherical constant', Zappa appreciated the travails of us linear, time-based mortals. And on 4 December 1993, Zappa's death from prostate cancer was a pretty definite 'end'. Yet his work endures, largely thanks to Rykodisc's decision to keep the entire catalogue on the racks, but also in repertoires both rockist (hello Muffin Men, hello Grandmothers) and classicising (hello Ensemble Modern, hello Britten Sinfonia). Meanwhile, composers Simon Fell, Dogbiz and Richard Hemmings show that Zappa's perverse eclecticism has kickstarted a genuine tradition.

What follows examines the albums in the sequence in which they were released (mostly), setting them against the fads and peer-group conformities they ridiculed – while at the same time respecting Zappa's 'conceptual continuity', his proposal that 'everything is actually happening all the time...'. Good luck.

Ben Watson, 1 April 1998

V6-5005-2
STEREO
Verve
The Mothers of Invention
FREAK OUT!

THE VERVE YEARS

FREAK OUT!

(ORIGINAL RELEASE: JULY 1966; CD RELEASE RYKODISC/RCD 10501)

When Frank Zappa made his debut, he had been active on the Hollywood music scene since graduating from High School in 1958. He'd scored movies (*The World's Greatest Sinner* and *Run Home Slow*), played in bars (both lounge music in cocktail bars and R&B in rough-houses) and finally found the musicians he needed with The Soul Giants (Roy Estrada on bass, Jimmy Carl Black on drums). He'd run his own studio in Cucamonga, producing novelty singles with singer Ray Collins and engineer Paul Buff ('Tijuana Surf' was a hit in Mexico) and much experimental over-dubbage on the then-new-and-untried multitrack tape-recorder. He'd also sold encyclopedias door-to-door and worked in the publicity department of a greetings-card firm. In other words, Zappa wasn't innocent of commercial manipulation; indeed his whole 'anti-commercial' schtick was predicated on the idea of how oppositional, non-conformist, freaky culture could attract attention and sell records.

Zappa's band The Mothers ('Of Invention' was added at record company insistence in order to disguise the – thoroughly intentional – connotation 'Motherfuckers') was signed by MGM's East Coast A&R Director Tom Wilson. One of Harvard's first black graduates, Wilson had produced both John Coltrane (a bizarre encounter with pianist Cecil Taylor) and the new, electrified, rock-'n'roll Bob Dylan (including the momentous 'Like A Rolling Stone'). When Wilson first caught The Mothers, guitarist Henry Vestine (later with Canned Heat) was aboard; they were playing an R&B number. However, Wilson warmed to Zappa's ambitions and secured $25,000 to make his first record, which was to be a double album ($6,000 was a more normal budget at the time). Zappa drafted in studio musicians and scene-setting freaks to augment an already powerful rock band. Zappa appreciated Wilson's commitment ('he laid his job on the line producing the album'); Wilson stayed with The Mothers until their fourth release (he can be seen in the front line of the famous Sgt. Pepper-parody crowd scene of *We're Only In It For The Money*).

Freak Out! was designed to inject a viral dose of intelligence, realism and antagonism into pop. Zappa had been impressed by the entry of Dylan's 'Like A Rolling Stone' into the charts. Like him, he wanted to wake up the youth, make them question the high-school rigmarole of saluting the flag and attending the Prom: practices which all seemed to lead to military service in Vietnam and returning in a body-bag. Zappa wanted to demolish the world subsequently depicted in *American Grafitti*. Music was his weapon: loud, twangy, full of mayhem and electric guitars. A solarized photograph showed The Mothers glowering on the cover, Zappa in a filthy-looking fur coat. On the back, a high-school virgin named 'Suzy Creamcheese' tells us the band is crazy and that they all smell bad.

Recording quality sounds refreshingly rude and crude today, but Zappa was actually making the music as sophisticated – albeit as offensive – as possible. On the opener, 'Hungry Freaks, Daddy', clamorous lead guitar replicated the distorted riff of the Stones' '(I Can't Get No) Satisfaction'. The lyrics point the finger at 'Mr America' and threaten a rising tide of non-conformism. Leering savagery threatens to capsize everything into cacophony. 'I Ain't Got No Heart' purported to summarise Zappa's 'feelings in social-sexual relationships', yet Ray Collins sounded eerily like a parody of Jim Morrison with The Doors (who were on the scene, but unsigned until later in the year). 'Who Are The Brain Police?', Zappa's ode to the authoritarian notion of thought crime, included a shocking moment of disorientation when Zappa dropped in a stretch of tape from a different recording (at 2.01). Like William Burroughs, Zappa was out to rattle his audience by splicing and subverting his technical means of representation. He wanted his listeners to question everything, including the 'authenticity' of his own art.

'Motherly Love' offered groupies a wild time. Since nothing was done to glamourize The Mothers – quite the opposite – the invitation explodes the usual hypocrisies that shelter teen pop and sexual matters. 'You're Probably Wondering Why I'm Here' is audience abuse as funny and provocative as anything by the Sex Pistols. A quote on the sleeve compared Zappa's approach to the 'absurd' plays of Samuel Beckett.

Zappa also included a quote by the avant-garde composer Edgard Varèse: 'The presentday composer refuses to die!'. Zappa was later to show that his understanding of Varèse's music was profound (despite namechecks by many contemporary composers, there is little 'classical' music today that isn't a retreat from Varèse's hardcore 1920s modernism). Zappa's trashing of commercial, top-ten pop was not simply destructive; what sounds like dadaist provocation – 'Help I'm A Rock' and 'The Return Of The Son Of Monster Magnet' – is also excellently-shaped modernist sound-composition (in other words, it repays repeated listening in a way that, say, 'Revolution No 9' on the Beatles' Double *White* does not).

One subtitle – 'Ritual Dance Of The Child Killer' – referred to the plot of Stravinsky's ballet *The Rite Of Spring*. But in this scandalous context, with 'Suzy Creamcheese' (played by Jeannie Vassoir) sounding as if she were simultaneously losing her virginity and having an orgasm (this was the 60s), nobody noticed. Exploding the requirements of taste (the 'good' pop song; the 'nice' arrangement; the 'serious' composition) allowed him to recombine social icons with the experimental excitement of the medieval alchemist (or, in Zappa's 50s pulp version, of the Mad Scientist clutching a test-tube of foaming goo). Outrage backed by conscientious, innovatory composition, *Freak Out!* previewed the music Zappa was to make for the rest of his life.

Inside the album's gatefold was a list of 184 names in eight columns of 23 (a number beloved of Aleister Crowley and William Burroughs). It provided the convert with a wealth of occasions for investigation and research. If *Freak Out*! had been all Zappa had ever released, it would have instigated a cult. As it was, it was just a start.

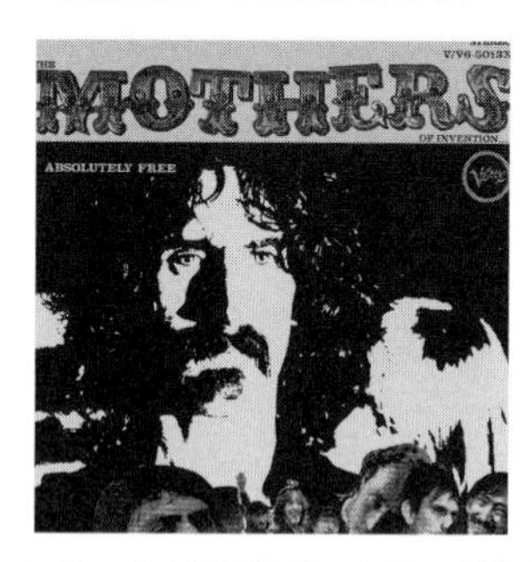

ABSOLUTELY FREE

(ORIGINAL RELEASE: APRIL 1967;
CD RELEASE RYKODISC/RCD 10502)

Freak Out! sold just 30,000 units; according to Zappa, MGM deemed it a flop. He was reduced to a budget of $11,000 for its successor. He lost Elliot Ingber – the quintessential underground/psychedelic guitarist resurfaced as Winged Eel Fingerling in Captain Beefheart's Magic Band – but he gained other musicians to add to his Estrada/Black rhythm section: drummer Billy Mundi, saxophonist Bunk Gardner and keyboardist Don Preston. The latter's father was resident composer for the Detroit Symphony; Preston grew up hearing the avantgarde classical music that inspired Zappa. He'd also played with John Coltrane's drummer Elvin Jones and toured with Nat King Cole. On top of that, he ran an avantgarde music club in LA: he, Gardner and Zappa had improvised there to films of microscopic pond life. Preston hadn't played on *Freak Out!* because he 'couldn't play rock'n'roll'. Now, after gigging with a few rock bands, he was ready to join Zappa – and take avantgarde music to the masses.

Absolutely Free is a more challenging record than *Freak Out!*. Instead of three 'freak out' tracks appended to a brace of (albeit parodic) rock/pop numbers, everything is woven into two suites. First-time listeners find it hard to believe that this wild melange of spoken-word, political wise-cracks and atonal (tuneless?) vocalising can become a favourite, but repeated listens reveal wonders. On the opener, Richard Berry's immortal 'Louie Louie' is used as a backing for a denunciation of the hypocrisies and repressions of straight America. 'The Duke Of Prunes' and 'Call Any Vegetable' are terrific melodies. Given the album's atmosphere of outrage, such felicities were rarely remarked. 'Invocation & Ritual Dance Of The Young Pumpkin' was Zappa's first extended guitar workout: over a static polychordal drone, he showed that he had thoroughly absorbed the lessons of his idols (Clarence 'Gatemouth' Brown and Johnny 'Guitar' Watson), transforming their rocking guitar breaks into a counter-cultural manifesto.

'The MOI American Pageant' (side two of the vinyl album) provided further indictment of the lameness of America. It still has no parallels for widescan awareness and indignant spleen. Musical motifs and verbal/political rhetoric are so brilliantly entwined it seems insufficient to call 'Brown Shoes Don't Make It' a 'song': bassoons, violins and electronics constructed a seething mosaic of contemporary ills (Zappa himself only achieved anything like it again in 1985, with 'Porn Wars'). A plethora of tape splices showed Zappa's awareness of musique concrète, the avant-garde music that appeared in Paris after the war where composers used tape-recorders to organize sound. Zappa regretted that primitive recording meant that many key exclamations from the closing portrayal of bar-room desperation were lost.

On the CD reissue, a contemporary single has been sequenced between the two suites: 'Big Leg Emma' b/w 'Why Don't You Do Me Right'. The latter is notable because of the cover made of it by Mark Perry's punk band ATV: rockist 'Louie Louie' dumbness transcends generational warfare. A pointed message in Zappa's cover collage – 'War Means Work For All', coupled with an atom-bomb mushroom (between the 'Y' of Absolutely and the 'F' of Free) – was originally toned down by MGM. In the shrunken graphic of the CD issue, it is illegible.

LUMPY GRAVY

(ORIGINAL RELEASE: MAY 1967; CD RELEASE RYKODISC/RCD 10504)

Lumpy Gravy has a special place in the Zappa oeuvre; he cited it as his favourite, and *Civilization Phaze III*, the magnum opus that occupied his last years, was meant to be its completion. It also constitutes Zappa's most extreme refusal of conventional formats. Although commissioned by Capitol Records to 'write something for an orchestra' – to the tune of $40,000 – Zappa also included eerily twee arrangements of jolly melodies, 30,000 bursts of guitar distortion, sped-up interludes, *musique concrète* and bizarre discussions by people who had been placed inside a piano. Whichever way you look at it, *Lumpy Gravy* was begging for commercial rejection. Although many of its procedures – collage, fragmentation, parody, humour, documentary – have since become requisites in the 'postmodern' academy, Zappa's formal writing was too brash and gutsy for contemporary classical recognition.

Lumpy Gravy's back cover showed Zappa – in tuxedo and top hat, his non-WASP, Mediterranean physiognomy leering into the camera – asking 'Is this phase 2 of We're Only In It For The Money?'. *Lumpy Gravy* was designed as a companion volume to the next release, working as its subtle, poetic, allusive counterpart (it even shares a small oasis of calm, romantic orchestration).

Towards the close we hear Zappa say 'Cos round things are... are boring.' Then he exhales, as if blowing out smoke. The listener is spiked with poetic discontent, pondering a list of 'round things' (smoke rings, circular logic, repetitive labour, records...). Despite his repeated condemnation of drugs, Zappa's dadaist attack on the workaday mundane was universally interpreted as dope-fuelled fantasy. In fact, no dope-head could summon the skill and energy to construct Zappa's surrealist monstrosity. When the slogan 'Round Things Are Boring' reappeared on the cover of *One Size Fits All* in 1975, Zappa's dedicated, no-detail-missed fans felt vindicated. Here was an art deliberately engineered to repay obsessive investigation. *Lumpy Gravy* appeared in the US album charts for just one week – at 159. Nevertheless, simply because of its refusal to be measured by any external standard, the album remains one of the great moments of Modern Art: a riot of intricately-crafted 'indulgence' that reproaches every time-serving orthodoxy, every time-server in the music biz.

WE'RE ONLY
IN IT FOR THE
MONEY

WE'RE ONLY IN IT FOR THE MONEY

(ORIGINAL RELEASE: SEPTEMBER 1968;
CD RELEASE RYKODISC/RCD 10503)

Whereas *Freak Out!* opened with an affront masquerading as a pop song, Money opens with a section of consummate musique concrète that sounds like a belch. Zappa immerses the listener in a sonic collage that guys the stuttering inarticulacy of the hippie subculture: '... er...', '... er...', 'are you hung up?', '... out-a-sight, yeah'. Zappa's satire is balm to the soul of anyone who has suffered drug-crippled fashion victims. Leon Trotsky argued that history-writing should be engaged, partisan: Zappa's portrayal of youth culture has a similar charge. He makes you take sides. At the height of Flower Power, when Allen Ginsberg's combination of never-never nirvana and lust-for-youth erotics had been embraced by The Beatles (and the editors of teen magazines all over the world), Zappa launched a barrage of objections.

Zappa always maintained that the freaks of LA were superior to the hippies of San Francisco. He was incensed that Jefferson Airplane and the Grateful Dead were hailed as countercultural heroes. According to him, their music 'wasn't even as funky as the little R&B combo I had in High School'. 'Who Needs The Peace Corps' ran through a list of Frisco clichés: Augustus Stanley Owsley III, the scene's acid-maker; the 'psychedelic dungeons' that were the hippie clubs; Bill Graham's celebrated venue, the Fillmore. Zappa's criticism of the hippies wasn't just grouchy: it was urgent and political. 'Concentration Moon' made warnings about the internment camps Richard Nixon was readying for non-conformists, while 'Mom & Dad' was a chilling premonition of how establishment forces would respond to the anti-war movement (in 1971, when the National Guard fired at protestors at Kent State University, Zappa's lyric became a bloody reality). 'Absolutely Free' mocked Flower Power by comparing its 'psychedelic' imagery to the names of the reindeer in Johnny Marks' banal seasonal hit 'Rudolf the Red Nosed Reindeer'.

Money concluded with 'The Chrome Plated Megaphone Of Destiny', an outrageous sonic-montage designed to outdo George Martin's 'mind-blowing' orchestration at the end of *Sgt. Pepper*. New Mother Ian Underwood was a prize-winning interpreter of Mozart; Zappa used his subtle touch for one of his own *études*. Yet the piano is recorded with such percussive realism it becomes as bizarre as the accompanying sped-up laughter and Stockhausen-like electronics (tamboura and koto twangs fed through oscillators and faders).

The covers of *Lumpy Gravy* and *We're Only In It For The Money* announced the arrival of Cal Schenkel, Zappa's most suggestive visual interpreter. Schenkel understood the dada aesthetic. He projected Zappa's interactive, multiplying detail onto the visual plane, providing countless motifs for the conceptual-continuity sleuth. His famous *Sgt. Pepper* parody was photographed by Jerrold Schatzberg in his New York studio; The Mothers were flanked by Tom Wilson on one side, and Jimi Hendrix on the other. A photo of manager Herbie Cohen's daughter Lisa was placed in Hendrix's arms. Frank's wife Gail, pregnant with daughter Moon Unit, wore a blue glitter dress. MGM's lawyers insisted on printing bars across the eyes of anyone in the collage who was still alive: their paranoia simply made it still more sinister. In the sleevenotes, Zappa advised listeners to read 'In The Penal Colony', a short story by Franz Kafka that dealt with homoerotic abuse, colonialism and military/judicial atrocity. *Money* remains a disturbing experience to this day.

STEREO
The Mothers Of Invention
Cruising with
RUBEN & THE JETS
IS THIS THE MOTHERS OF INVENTION RECORDING UNDER A DIFFERENT NAME IN A LAST DITCH ATTEMPT TO GET THEIR CRUDDY MUSIC ON THE RADIO?
QUACKQUACK
SNAT

CRUISING WITH RUBEN & THE JETS

(ORIGINAL RELEASE: NOVEMBER 1968;
CD RELEASE RYKODISC/RCD 10505)

In the midst of opening up pop to every subversive manifestation of modern culture, Zappa recorded an album of retrospective nostalgia. It harked back to the doo-wop of the 50s. *Ruben & The Jets*, he declared, was constructed in the spirit of Stravinsky's neo-classical works ('Fountain Of Love' faded out on a riff derived from *The Rite Of Spring*): a simulacrum. Cal Schenkel's graphics reinforced the sense of schizophrenia: a photograph of The Mothers shatters to reveal an impersonal universe of Victorian plumbing, printed circuits and space-rocket attachments.

Zappa toyed with the idea of deliberately scratchy, lo-fi sound, but settled for compressed sonorities that emphasize the mechanical nature of the music. On 'Stuff Up The Cracks', the singer gases himself. The whole record is about claustrophobia and asphyxiation. As a voice says on 'Later That Night': 'there's no room to breathe in here'. This applied to both the closeted 50s mentality and the restricted nature of the music.

Ruben & The Jets is the only Zappa album that critic Greil Marcus has time for. Though this demonstrates the perils of allowing Dylanologists to voice musical judgments, it does prove that *Ruben* is more than condescending parody. When legendary Zappologist Danny Houston bought the record, he went home and cried his eyes out to it. Cemented inside the paper-thin walls of *Ruben*'s satirical multitracks there is a layer of genuine doo-wop soul. Vocalist Ray Collins never sang better.

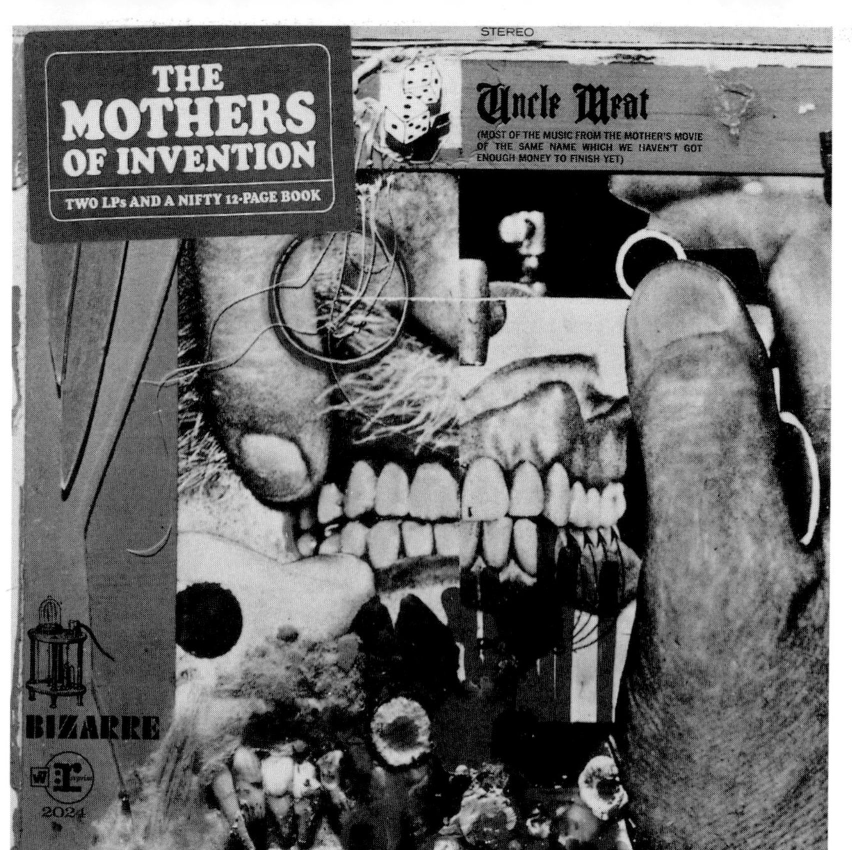
STEREO
THE
MOTHERS
OF INVENTION
TWO LPs AND A NIFTY 12-PAGE BOOK
Uncle Meat
(MOST OF THE MUSIC FROM THE MOTHER'S MOVIE
OF THE SAME NAME WHICH WE HAVEN'T GOT
ENOUGH MONEY TO FINISH YET)
BIZARRE
2024

UNCLE MEAT

(ORIGINAL RELEASE: MARCH 1969;
CD RELEASE RYKODISC/RCD 10506/07)

Zappa was still printing Edgard Varèse's quote on his albums – 'The presentday composer refuses to die!' – but so far his talent for outrage had obscured his skills as a composer. *Uncle Meat* aimed to set that right, a double-vinyl release that downplayed lyrics. 'Basically this is an instrumental album', it said inside the gatefold. A note described the technique of overdubbing, which was used extensively, opening up the weird world of virtual orchestration. New recruits Art Tripp and Ruth Komanoff (later Underwood) were classically-trained percussionists. They helped Zappa realise some of his fiendish metrical ingenuities. Ian Underwood played harpsichord: a jangling, absurdist quality infuses all the music. *Uncle Meat* became a great favourite in Europe, and almost singlehandedly gave birth to the genre Art Rock. Although Canterbury Rock and Henry Cow might have fused Stravinsky, rock and 'pataphysical' absurdity without Zappa's example, it seems unlikely. Fred Frith cites 'Nine Types Of Industrial Pollution' as an inspiration, especially for the way the guitar was recorded.

One-time house-mate Pamela Zarubica appeared as the 'Voice Of The Cheese'. Zappa takes the listener from domestic intimacy to rock-venue spectacle in breathtaking lurches. On *Lumpy Gravy* spoken word segued into music as if notes were expressions of the subverbal; on *Uncle Meat* the cleavage between private and public becomes glaring. A live recording of Don Preston playing 'Louie Louie' on the Royal Albert Hall organ – to wild applause – symbolised every desecration Zappa wished to perpetrate on old-world values. For good measure, The Mothers also murdered 'God Bless America' (an equivalent statement to the distortions Hendrix was applying to 'Star Spangled Banner').

'The Air' had lyrics about customs searches and tape recordings. Drummer Jimmy Carl Black can be heard bitching about band policy and pay. On an early version of *Uncle Meat* aired on German radio, Black can be heard saying 'Is that thing on?'. Zappa answers 'No'. This exchange was omitted on the final release, but it showed Zappa's awareness of the power relations of recording. As Zappologist Jonathan Jones has pointed out, this was appropriate in a period that culminated in Watergate and the impeachment of a US president on the basis of illicit tape-recordings.

On the original vinyl, side four was occupied by six different versions of 'King Kong' (Zappa's splendid 3/8 ode to the abused gorilla). This became a regular feature of his double-vinyl albums: a concluding side of 'music music'. For CD reissue, to make it a double-disc release, half-an-hour of the soundtrack of *Uncle Meat* was added. This detracts from the album's lustrous statistical density (those wishing to experience *Uncle Meat* in its original form should program disc two from 'King Kong Itself' onward). Gratifyingly, the CD-reissue includes a reprint of the original booklet, with such essential items as the scores for 'Uncle Meat' and 'King Kong', a diagram of a doll foot as a young rifle, references to Captain Beefheart's contemporaneous masterpiece *Trout Mask Replica*, plus Zappa's first foray into science fiction: speculation about how the media dictate our sense of time. Beneath Zappa's B-movie clichés boils a Burroughs-like paranoia.

FRANK ZAPPA

HOT RATS

THE BIZARRE YEARS

HOT RATS

(ORIGINAL RELEASE: OCTOBER 1969;
CD RELEASE RYKODISC/RCD 10508)

Zappa's contract with MGM expired at the end of 1968. In March 1969, Zappa and manager Herbie Cohen set up Bizarre Records. This gave them control over music and packaging, but they needed a major for distribution: they chose Reprise, Frank Sinatra's label, which had recently been acquired by Warner Brothers. Like *Lumpy Gravy*, *Hot Rats* was a solo record credited to Frank Zappa. However, it dispensed with dada disruption in favour of hard-driving tunes and state-of-the-art production. Using a 16-track recorder for the first time, Zappa later said the album was 'more about over-dubbing than anything else' (the CD reissue replaced some overdubs vinyl could not cope with). It was a hit in England, where it became Zappa's most famous record – the 'interruptions' provided by his lyrics and spoken word had been barriers to his acceptance (this helps explain Zappa's cult following in Europe; for non-English speakers, his words are less disruptive).

Ruben & The Jets showed that the roots of rock'n'roll ran deeper than a few Chuck Berry songs. The jazz-rock of *Hot Rats* also dug deep. Zappa called upon some of the great musicians of the West Coast. In the late 50s, violinist Don 'Sugarcane' Harris had been part of a duo called Don & Dewey, recording Little Richard-style R&B fire-crackers for the Specialty label. Bassist Max Bennett was a veteran of the Hollywood studios; he had played with Shorty Rogers, Vic Feldman and Quincy Jones, toured with Peggy Lee. John Guerin was a young drummer who had been working with Tom Scott on fusing rock and jazz. Paul Humphrey had drummed for Wes Montgomery, Gene Ammons and Lee Konitz. In other words, Zappa supplied himself with the finest rhythm section money could buy. The other important presence on the record was Ian Underwood, who contributed reeds and keyboards. Jazz critics objected to his untutored sound, but his snorting sax is fresh and pokesome.

The lyrics of 'Willie The Pimp' derived from an interview Zappa conducted with a New York-based groupie named Annie (included on the Mystery Disc of *The Old Masters* Box Two – see 'Collectables' in the Appendix). It starts with a lascivious, growling vocal from Captain Beefheart and blues-drenched violin from Sugarcane. Zappa then plunges into a classic guitar solo. His wah-wah pedal made the notes talk, while his sense of melody evokes a yearning melancholy amidst all the frenzy. On the rest, perverse tunes kept the unisons buoyant, while Zappa's grasp of film-music orchestration provided exotic harmonies. Ian Underwood's 'organus maximus' was actually a pipe organ. Zappa dubbed in percussion – chains, castanets – to provide extra sizzle. On 'Gumbo Variations', the music whistles like a pressure cooker: a new slant on the jazz idea of 'cookin''. On the cover, Christine Frka of the GTOs lurked inside a disused swimming pool: a striking image that was seen under many an arm in the heady days of the early 70s.

STEREO
THE
MOTHERS
OF INVENTION
7
5
BIZARRE
REPRISE
RS 6370
BURNT
WEENY
SANDWICH

BURNT WEENY SANDWICH

(ORIGINAL RELEASE: DECEMBER 1969; CD RELEASE RYKODISC/RCD 10509)

Burnt Weeny Sandwich is indeed a sandwich, a dollop of Zappa composition between two slices of trivia: 'WPLJ' (a jingle for White Port and Lemon Juice), and a cover of 'Valarie' by Jackie & The Starlites (the way the lead singer breaks down in tears on the original must be heard to be believed). According to writer Barry Miles, Johnny Otis – the Godfather of R&B – led The Mothers through Zappa's scores, while the composer oversaw the recording in the control booth. Otis was actually clapping in Roy Estrada's face, who didn't appreciate his help! Echo and out-of-tune playing were deployed to achieve a 'greasy' feel.

'Igor's Boogie' was written for Stravinsky, while 'Holiday in Berlin' was for the militant German students who had staged a stage invasion in October 1968, demanding that Zappa make an anti-capitalist statement (Zappa later said their leaders wanted him to tell the audience to burn down a nearby American forces base). 'Aybe Sea' was a tinkling piano *étude* that again relied on Ian Underwood's sensitive touch: on the vinyl, his meditations finish side one and are resumed on side two. Sound is raw and sprawling compared to *Hot Rats*. Sugarcane's solo on 'The Little House I Used to live in' is an awesome electric storm, while Zappa's organ solo recalls the pipe-band 'rudiments' he learned as a twelve-year-old in Keith McKillop's percussion class back in 1952.

KING KONG
JEAN-LUC PONTY
PLAYS THE MUSIC OF
FRANK ZAPPA
MUSIC FOR ELECTRIC VIOLIN AND LOW BUDGET ORCHESTRA COMPOSED AND ARRANGED BY FRANK ZAPPA

KING KONG: JEAN-LUC PONTY PLAYS THE MUSIC OF FRANK ZAPPA

(ORIGINAL RELEASE: JANUARY 1970;
CD RELEASE CAPITAL/BLUE NOTE CDP077778953920)

A delightful collection of jazz humouresques. The violinist was accompanied by excellent musicians: Art Tripp and John Guerin played drums, Buell Neidlinger (ex-Cecil Taylor) and Wilton Felder (moonlighting from The Crusaders) bass. Zappa contributed wah-wah guitar to a Ponty composition, and Ian Underwood conducted 'Music For Electric Violin And Low Budget Orchestra' (named after Pacific Records turned down Zappa's request for a 97-piece orchestra). Ponty later fell out with Zappa, but at this date his background in classical music and the Parisian experimental scene was mightily congruent. The record was also notable for the elegant chording of Cannonball Adderley's pianist George Duke, who formed a jazz-rock band with Ponty and then joined The Mothers. Leonard Feather, doyen of jazz critics, contributed urbane liner notes.

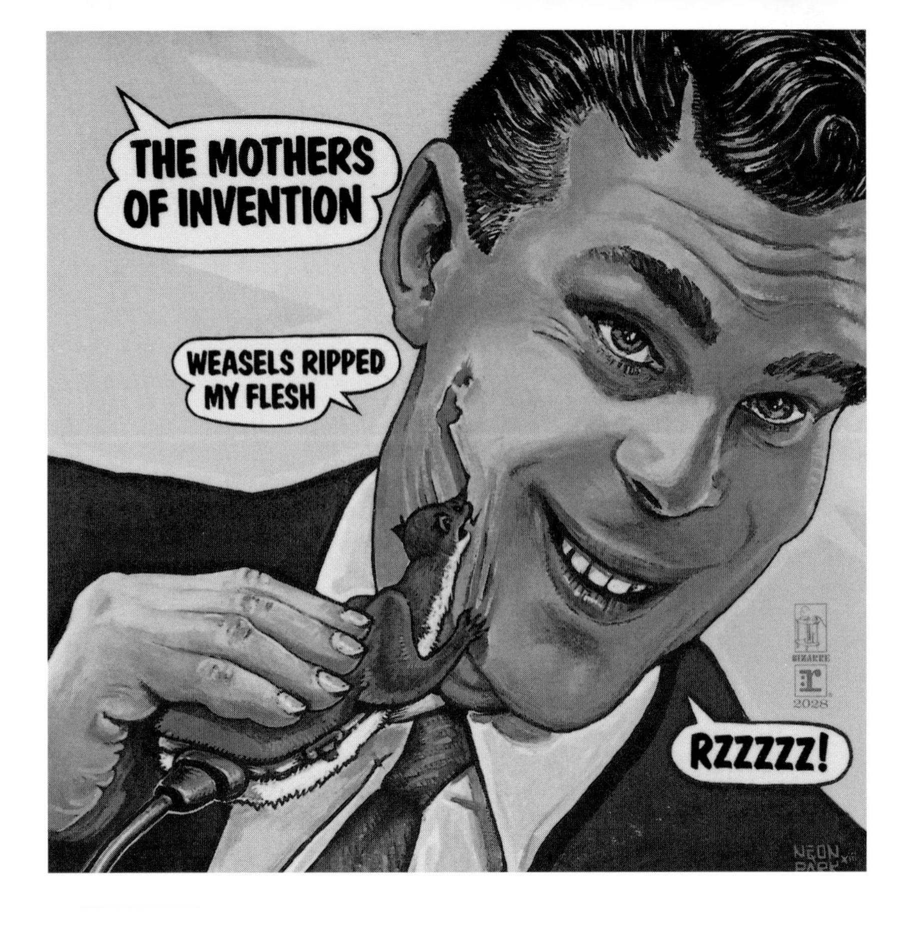
THE MOTHERS OF INVENTION
WEASELS RIPPED MY FLESH
RZZZZZ!
BIZARRE
2028
NEON PARK

WEASELS RIPPED MY FLESH

(ORIGINAL RELEASE: FEBRUARY 1970;
CD RELEASE RYKODISC/RCD 10510)

Weasels was originally designed as a sampler for a 12-record set, 'The History & Collected Improvisations Of The Mothers Of Invention'. It collated live and studio recordings, demonstrating that, for Zappa, heavy R&B – Sugarcane's performance of Little Richard's 'Directly From My Heart To You' is consummate – was part of the same sonic universe as the avantgarde orchestral music of Edgard Varèse and the weirded-out jazz of Eric Dolphy. The latter was given his own 'Memorial Barbecue', a stunning encounter between bizarre harmonies and electronic distortion.

Weasels also featured another notorious sleeve, a hilariously gruesome painting by Neon Park (Martin Muller from San Francisco). When guitarist Lowell George – who can be heard imitating a Gestapo officer on 'Didja Get Any Onya' – broke away to form Little Feat, he insisted on using Neon Park for all their covers. The title of 'Prelude To The Afternoon Of A Sexually Aroused Gas Mask' nodded to Debussy's ballet about the skipping faun, but the heavy-rock sounds were totally The Mothers. 'My Guitar Wants To Kill Your Mama' is an icon of teenage rebellion, so deftly executed it feels like parody. This distancing was designed to upset notions of rock as self expression, to isolate social attitudes so that they might be examined in the light of reason. This self-consciousness was starting to annoy the critics.

The title track was simply two minutes and seven seconds of feedback. It would be many years later – with the advent of Lo-Fi and 'noise' bands like Sonic Youth – that such strategies would become familiar to rock listeners. As it was, Zappa was happy to be known as the King Of Weird: it gave him carte blanche to employ any musical texture or style that took his fancy.

CHUNGA'S REVENGE

(ORIGINAL RELEASE: OCTOBER 1970;
CD RELEASE RYKODISC/RCD 10511)

Chunga's Revenge introduced singers Flo & Eddie (ex-Turtles Mark Volman and Howard Kaylan, a duo who later sang backing vocals for T Rex), an indication that Zappa would not only employ musicians to supplement the Mothers Of Invention, but new singers and personalities too (a crime 'original Mothers fans' never forgave).

Aynsley Dunbar – who had accompanied Merseybeat legend Freddie Starr, English bluesmen John Mayall and Jeff Beck, and covered 'Willie The Pimp' on his *Blue Whale* album – provided hard-driving yet fluid drums very different from either Black's heavy stomp or the tricky time playing of Tripp and Komanoff. 'Transylvania Boogie' was appropriately named, as Zappa gloried in gypsy harmonies and worked the wah-wah pedal. 'Twenty Small Cigars', a *Hot Rats* out-take, had a haunting cool-jazz quality. 'The Nancy & Mary Music' featured George Duke's 'vocal drum imitations', his own version of The Mothers' ludicrous vocalese. As usual, Zappa ploughed a creative furrow between burlesque and experiment. The title track had Sugarcane Harris playing organ, while Ian Underwood put his alto sax through a wah-wah pedal. The weird, whingeing, claustrophobic tone that resulted was surely the inspiration for Zappa's cover concept: a 'mutant industrial vacuum cleaner' dancing about a 'mysterious night time camp fire' with castanets 'clutched by the horrible suction of its heavy duty hose'. Zappa's wife Gail cites the album's title as proof of Frank's prescience – at the time he had no idea that La Chunga was a leading flamenco singer.

The vocal tracks made socio-political observations about rock hysteria, sexual frustration and male violence (both military and that of gun-slinging union mafiosi). Zappa's laboratory examples of pop star behaviour – Volman and Kaylan – were placed under a surrealist microscope: a preview of the film *200 Motels*. 'Road Ladies' detailed the pleasures and diseases to be derived from groupies ('don't you better get a shot from the doctor'). The same medical issue provided a title for a brilliant snippet of cartoon-Varèse percussion executed by Zappa – 'The Clap'.

FILLMORE EAST JUNE 1970

**(ORIGINAL RELEASE: AUGUST 1971;
CD RELEASE RYKODISC/RCD 10512)**

For the cover of *Fillmore East June 1970*, Cal Schenkel was told to scribble the title on plain white cardboard in pencil ('he made me do it' he put after his credit on the back). The music, too, was rude and raw, forty minutes of rock recorded live at Bill Graham's New York venue. Zappa maintained that, rather than any particular notes or rhythms, timbre (the quality of sound) defined rock. He proved it here with new versions of 'Little House I Used To Live In', 'Willie The Pimp' and 'Peaches En Regalia': the band's raucous, fuzzed, power-chord amplitude makes them completely different from the bizarro jazz of *Sandwich* and *Rats*. Volman and Kaylan performed a vaudeville routine that circulated underground-rock folklore about groupies: the one who insisted that before she'd get into bed, the pop star sing his hit; salacious games played with mudsharks and octopuses fished out of a window at Seattle's Edgewater Inn. As usual, outrage about 'obscenity' tended to overshadow the musical quality of this truly 'rocking' combo.

Likewise, the band's seamless velocity makes it easy to miss quite how subtle and complex compositions like 'Little House', 'Latex Solar Beef' and 'Peaches' actually are (the great respect for Zappa among musicians can be ascribed to the fact that the chords and rhythms he uses, even for his so-called 'comedy' tunes, are invariably non-standard). Don Preston's moog solo on 'Lonesome Electric Turkey' was a mini-symphony of avantgarde electronics. A vinyl 7" single of the last track, 'Tears Began To Fall', was issued at this time, with a guitar solo on the flipside named 'Junior Mintz Boogie' (for some reason, both tunes were credited to 'Billy Dexter'). Unfortunately, this stray gem wasn't included on the CD, and worse,

'Willie The Pimp Part Two' (on vinyl, side one finished in the middle of this terrific guitar solo; it resumed once the record had been turned over) was also omitted.

Conceptual-continuity sleuths will be pleased to note the reoccurence of words from 'Latex Solar Beef' – 'see the screaming/hot black steaming/ iridescent naugahyde python gleaming/steam roller' – in 'Stick It Out' on *Joe's Garage* eight years later (this time, due to the presence of a lyric-sheet, this erotico-kaballistic incantation can be deciphered). John Lennon and Yoko Ono appeared on stage with The Mothers at this concert (6 June 1971); some of the resulting mayhem appeared on a Phil Spector-produced insert in *Some Time In New York City*. Listeners used to Zappa's premium production values would have to wait until 1992's *Playground Psychotics* to distentangle Yoko Ono's primal screams from Zappa's rabid guitar.

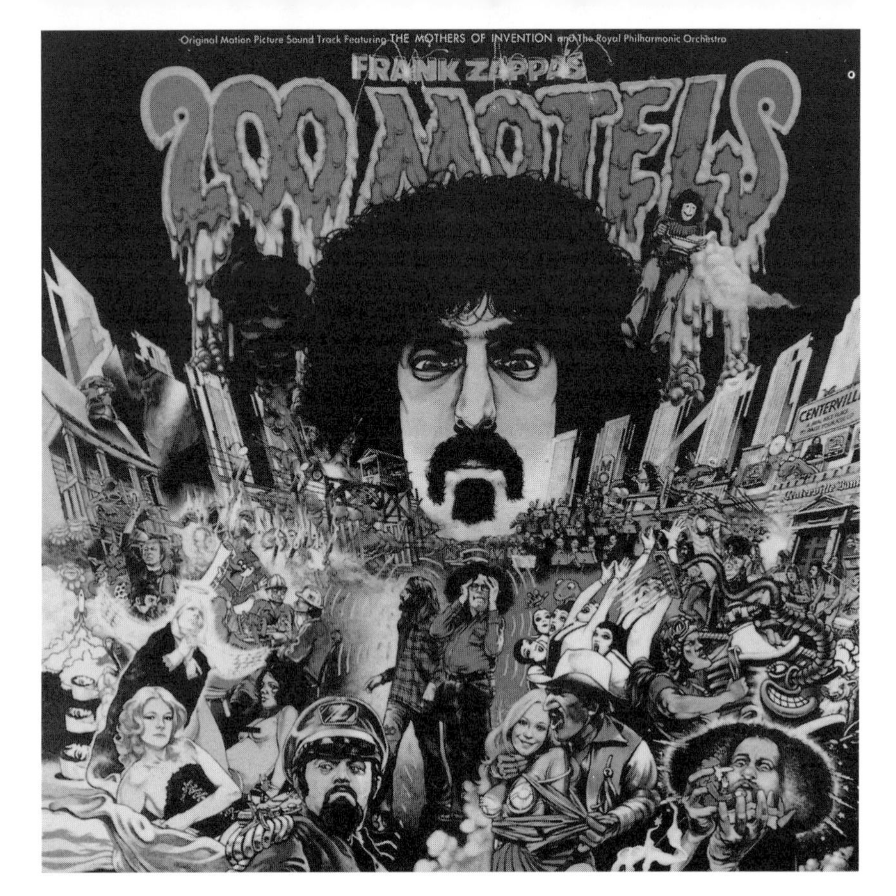
Original Motion Picture Sound Track Featuring THE MOTHERS OF INVENTION and The Royal Philharmonic Orchestra
FRANK ZAPPA'S
200 MOTELS
CENTERVILL

200 MOTELS

(ORIGINAL RELEASE: OCTOBER 1971;
CD RELEASE RYKODISC/RCD 10513/14)

Zappa was pleasantly surprised by the $630,000 budget offered him by United Artists for his first feature film. He decided to make it in England and take advantage of the Royal Philharmonic Orchestra: at £1,000 a day for a 100-musician orchestra, it would enable him to hear a significant amount of the orchestral music he had been writing on tour. Almost universally panned by film critics for 'self-indulgence' – narrative chaos and in-jokes – *200 Motels* is actually a 'surrealist documentary' of the experience of being on tour. Writing retrospectively in *Avant* magazine, dada-composer Richard Hemmings – too young to be outraged at the addition of Flo & Eddie to the Mothers – hailed it as a work of 'social anthropology'. Germany's premier jazz critic, Joachim Berendt, called the film 'an especially revealing example of dressing up highly developed intellectuality in the style of a bizarre, contemporary Don Quixote'.

200 Motels also works as an album. Zappa's music has always been about the collision of social attitudes and genres. The physical presence in Pinewood Studios of a symphony orchestra and genuine 'pop stars' (Volman and Kaylan, along with Ringo Starr as 'Larry The Dwarf', Keith Moon as nun and trainee groupie, and drummer Aynsley Dunbar) allowed him to make the collision palpable. On the record, these forces are manifested in magnificent segues between string-orchestra sensitivity and hard-rock fury. 'Magic Fingers' showed that Zappa had been listening to Black Sabbath; the fact that his scores were finally being interpreted by a 'proper' orchestra seemed to push him to the opposite extreme in his song-writing. The descending riff and his own live-on-screen guitar solo detonated new depths of heaviness.

An orchestral version of 'Holiday In Berlin' from *Burnt Weeny Sandwich* provides the 'semi-fraudulent/direct-from-Hollywood overture'. The original introduction – Ringo's speech about how the rock revolution has 'putrified' the minds of the young and meant retraining orchestral musicians for the modern world – is reduced to compère Theodore Bikel telling us that Larry The Dwarf is 'dressed up like Frank Zappa' (in the film, Ringo was dangled on the end of a wire like a puppet). 'Mystery Roach' detailed drug/road fatigue ('What are we singing about?... We must be flipping out...'), while 'This Town Is A Sealed Tuna Sandwich' is a Brechtian portrayal of the sordidness and tedium of the modern metropolis.

Jimmy Carl Black played the part of 'Lonesome Cowboy Burt' – the hippie-hating redneck – with particular glee, the irony being that he's a Cherokee Indian (you also hear George Duke supplying uproarious trombone). 'Would You Like A Snack', 'Centerville', 'She Painted Up Her Face', 'Half A Dozen Provocative Squats' and 'Shove It Right In' described band and groupies as they prepared to meet each other. The music has a vaudeville feel that was anathema to the heavy-rock sensibility, but the bathos was thoroughly intentional: Zappa was documenting the reality behind the stagey megalomania of the likes of Led Zeppelin. In the film, 'Lucy's Seduction Of A Bored Violinist' used video technology to project Lucy Oferall's erotic gesticulations over the obedient arm-movements of an RPO violinist. In this satire, no-one was left off the hook.

'I'm Stealing The Towels' and 'Dental Hygiene Dilemma' were the soundtrack to Cal Schenkel's animations, emphasising the affinity Zappa's music has for cartoons, with its swiftness, violence, humour, and contempt for bourgeois-realist 'depth'. 'Daddy, Daddy, Daddy' was as tender a song as Zappa ever wrote, describing the allure of a confident groupie for sex-starved musicians. 'Penis Dimension' mocked male anxieties over the size of the esteemed organ, and 'What Will This Evening Bring Me This Morning' brought out the poignant contingency of sexual encounter. All this music was tightly organized, with Flo & Eddie's vocals soaring over complex orchestrations. If the film hadn't been also been a barrage of jokes, absurdism and seeming chaos, it would have been hailed as 'rock opera'.

'A Nun Suit Painted On Some Old Boxes' took absurdity to new heights, as a trained soprano sang an atonal aria to Moterhead Sherwood whilst enclosing him in a series of cardboard boxes (painted with a nun-suit). It all turns out to be a dream dremt by Keith Moon-as-nun-and-trainee-groopie. Arnold Schoenberg's *Pierrot Lunaire* (written in 1912) is taken to be the founding work of atonality. Paying homage to the moon-touched lunacy of *Pierrot Lunaire* by boxing Keith Moon is a classic example of Zappa's 'prescience'.

At the end of 'Magic Fingers', Howard Kaylan's monologue about his sexual cravings expresses everything that high-classical 'seriousness' represses. The lyrics of 'The Girl Wants To Fix Him Some Broth' and 'Little Green Sweaters & Corduroy Ponce' (titles that make most rock songs seem verbally destitute) anticipate the word-play of Zappa's mid-70s songs. A note to *Uncle Meat* said the lyrics were 'scientifically prepared from a random series of syllables, dreams, neuroses and private jokes'. Jokes, dreams and neuroses were all used by Sigmund Freud to track down the operations of the unconscious. When the soprano sings 'Broth reminds me of nuns, I see them smashing kids with rulers...', Zappa is free-associating, allowing random connections to open up his memory-banks (in this case, painful memories of his Catholic schooling). At the conclusion, 'Strictly Genteel' tells the audience to 'reach out your hand to/the girl in the dog book'; 'have mercy on... the dykes and the weird little children they grow'; 'help everybody/so they all get some action/some love on the weekend/some real satisfaction'. Zappa's idea of the politics of rock was not propaganda, but a liberation of unconscious desires, an assault on censorship both personal and public.

The film ends in a close-up of Zappa's

eyeball, as Howard Kaylan says 'he is the guy that is making me do all this shit...'. Zappa's wager was that unbridled 'self-indulgence' on his part would outwit the censorship of mundane commonsense, thus encouraging anti-authoritarian wish-fulfillment on the part of his audience. This dadaist strategy impressed few film citics, but Zappa fans were granted music that alternated rock and orchestral timbres with a new, garish intensity.

Rykodisc's CD-reissue was long delayed. *200 Motels* belonged to United Artists, the sole mastertape Zappa failed to secure in his lifetime. When the package arrived, it was deluxe, including CD-ROM-playable versions of Schenkel's cinema trailers, a fold-out film poster (showing Ringo Starr dressed up to look like Frank Zappa) and a painstaking, fact-packed essay on the making of the film by Patrick Pending.

JUST ANOTHER BAND FROM L.A.

(ORIGINAL RELEASE: MAY 1972;
CD RELEASE RYKODISC/RCD 10515)

On 20 December 1971, a member of the audience named Trevor Howell propelled himself into rock's hall of fame by pushing Zappa off the fifteen-foot stage at London's Rainbow. Zappa sustained a skull fracture, a twisted neck, a broken wrist and leg, and a paralysed arm. He was confined to a wheelchair for a year.

During that time he refused interviews and photo sessions, but he did manage to produce three albums. The first had been recorded live at Pauley Pavilion, UCLA, on 7 August 1971, using Zappa's latest acquisition, a Scully 4-track tape-recorder. *Just Another Band From LA* documented the kind of concerts 'Las Mothers' (as they were billed on the cover) were performing until Zappa's accident. The programme is helter-skelter rock vaudeville featuring Flo & Eddie with outbreaks of scabrous guitar. 'Billy The Mountain' is a 24-minute radio play with musical interludes and effects. A mountain and his tree-girlfriend Ethel defy the forces of the establishment represented by Studebacher Hoch. The lyrics were a patchwork of media trivia, with jingles from local TV and jokes about LA fastfood chains.

One critic claimed he fell in love with Zappa's art as soon as he heard the words 'the influence of a frozen beef pie'. Others were less enamoured. A sinister string of verbal associations – 'January, February, March, July, Wednesday, August, Irwindale, 2:30 In The Afternoon, Sunday, Walnut, Funny Cars, City Of Industry, Big John Masmanian...' – reappeared on the starmap on the back of *One Size Fits All*. The omission of Masmanian, a Watergate conspirator, only made conceptual-continuity paranoids still more excited. Ordinary folk, on the other hand, generally found 'Billy The Mountain' yet another example of unlistenable self-indulgence.

However, those who dismissed *Just Another Band* missed gems. 'Call Any Vegetable' turned *Absolutely Free*'s hymn to freakish enlightenment into an adrenalin-spiked anthem bursting with rockist energy. Zappa's guitar solo on this and 'Dog Breath' (from *Uncle Meat*) were caterwauling triumphs of amplified excess. 'Magdalena' was the true story of a Canadian girl who'd left home because she'd been sexually assaulted by her dad. Howard Kaylan's talk-over – voicing the desperation and confusion of her 'straight' father – is all the more shocking two decades later, now that child-abuse provides regular headline material. The father's sad fantasies replay the satire of Nabokov's *Lolita*. Whitebread nuclear-family America was still hurting, and Zappa wasn't going to let anyone forget it.

HOT RATS: WAKA/JAWAKA

(ORIGINAL RELEASE: JULY 1972; CD RELEASE RYKODISC/RCD 10516)

Still wheelchair-bound, Zappa took his musicians into Paramount Studios. On the 17-minute 'Big Swifty', overdubbing allowed Zappa to turn a sextet into a virtual big band. Aynsley Dunbar's drumming supplied polyrhythmic fluency, aided by Alex Dmochowski, his English bassist (playing under the name 'Erroneous'). The closing theme was a Zappa guitar solo transcribed by trumpeter Sal Marquez and arranged for brass (live versions appear on the first two volumes of *You Can't Do That On Stage Anymore*).

Electric instruments soloing over a rock beat invited comparisons to Miles Davis and John McLaughlin, but there is an ironical twist to the tunes that makes the music undeniably Zappaesque. George Duke's splendid keyboards and Sal Marquez's muted-trumpet wittering also have a humorous quality. Whereas contemporary jazz rock was reaching out to the cosmos, Zappa kept everything low-key and humorous.

'Your Mouth' is a tale of psychotic male jealousy ('you might loose a bunch of teeth... my shot gun... just might want to blow you away'), but sung in a deceptively light style (and with a killer country slide-guitar solo by Tony Duran). 'It Just Might Be A One-Shot Deal' describes someone hallucinating and advises them to dig it 'while it's happening': according to Zappa's Zen-tinged materialism, life is no rehearsal. Jeff Simmons, who had recorded a brilliant album of psychedelic balladry for Zappa's Straight label – *Lucille Has Messed My Mind Up* – sang and played Hawaiian guitar.

'Waka/Jawaka' has a cantering cowboy rhythm. Don Preston delivers a lyrical, almost pastoral solo on mini-moog that develops a crazy, cuboid relationship to the underlying metre. Again, Zappa's decisive mix locks the notes in, so that even though Preston was improvising, everything has a classical tightness. As the theme fades out accompanied by orchestral chimes, Ravel's *Bolero* is evoked. Although a commercial non-starter, *Waka/Jawaka* is a great favourite among jazz fans who are open-minded enough to give Zappa a listen.

THE
GRAND
WAZOO
MYSTERY HORN

THE GRAND WAZOO

(ORIGINAL RELEASE: DECEMBER 1972;
CD RELEASE RYKODISC/RCD 10517)

The Grand Wazoo brought many of the musical ideas of *Waka/Jawaka* to fruition, as well as supplying the images and storyline that invariably buttress a major Zappa production.

Zappa knew this music wasn't commercial: when he organized a tour for the small orchestra that would play his charts, he announced ahead of time when it would disband. Zappa drafted in a team of West Coast jazz and session players – including saxophonist Ernie Watts, later to play the sultry instrumental on the flipside of 'You're The One That I Want' by John Travolta and Olivia Newton-John – but he retained the Dmochowski/Dunbar rhythm section from *Waka/Jawaka*. Although they subdivide the beat most skillfully, they keep steady time, creating a sophisto-rock lushness that has found few exponents (violinist Billy Bang's *Fire From Within* on Black Saint, 1984, and saxist Bobby Zankel's *Prayer And Action* on CIMP, 1996, are rare exceptions).

'The Grand Wazoo' has an extended muted-trumpet solo from Sal Marquez; 'Cletus Awreetus-Awrightus' (named after Big Joe Turner's 'All right then! All reet then!' routine) has a superbly silly vocal from Zappa as he reveals the infantile, 'mouth-noise' source of his brass arrangement; 'Eat That Question' is introduced by glorious George Duke keyboard stylings (transcribed and reproduced by Mike Keneally for the 1988 tour version on *Make A Jazz Noise Here*). The song describes the treatment dealt out to a 'grotesque cult of masochistic ascetic fanatics who don't like music' – instead of feeding Christians to the lions, this Funky Emperor, feeds Questions to an acquarium-ful of UDT (UnDifferentiated Tissue, a concept Zappa borrowed from William Burroughs' 'talking asshole' routine). The portrayal of the UDT gulping down the questions gives Zappa's musicians a chance to indulge in some of the motifs that signified Panthalassa (or the 'primordial ocean') for contemporary fusion players.

The album closes with a restful, idyllic tune; appropriately enough, after all the preceding musical agitation, it was called 'Blessed Relief'. Jazz writer Joachim Berendt hailed *The Grand Wazoo* as the 'culmination point' of Zappa's music, but Zappa was already professing impatience with the kind of musicians required to play his complex charts. He did not appreciate the fact that they preferred playing chess to chasing groupies and getting laid ('Po-Jama People' on *One Size Fits All* was written for them). For Zappa's brand of 'amateur anthropology' to work, he needed musicians prepared to go 'out there' socially and sexually, as well as musically. On the cover of *The Grand Wazoo*, the logo of Bizarre Records can be seen being toppled from its plinth by the army of Mediocrites Of Pedestrium. Herbie Cohen and Frank Zappa were indeed planning to close down Bizarre and set up a new label for the 70s. Again referencing Big Joe Turner's catch-phrase, it was to be called DiscReet.

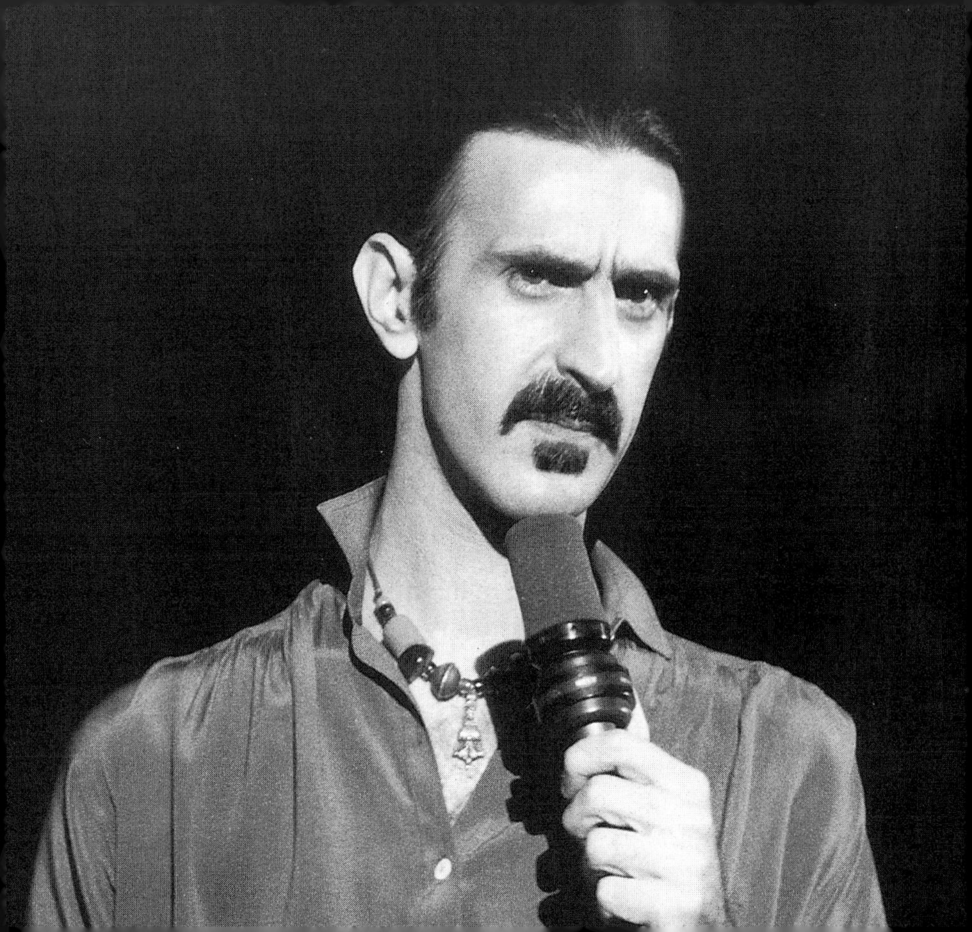

DISCREET
ZAPPA/
MOTHERS
STAGE PASS
AIR-INDIA
STAGE PASS
Florida
Over-nite Sensation
David B. McMacken
MCMLXXIII

OVER-NITE SENSATION

(ORIGINAL RELEASE: JUNE 1973; CD RELEASE RYKODISC/RCD 10518)

Over-Nite Sensation launched an edition of The Mothers that became legendary: a funky rhythm section (Ralph Humphrey on drums and Tom Fowler on bass) was complemeted by two experienced electric jazzers (George Duke on keyboards, Jean-Luc Ponty on violin), two great brass players (Bruce Fowler on trombone and Sal Marquez on trumpet) and the freaky, classically-honed talents of Ruth and Ian Underwood (percussion and woodwinds respectively). Songs were calculatedly lewd, rude and crazy, delivered with rampaging intensity and recorded with hair-raising clarity. *Over-Nite Sensation* quickly entered the US album charts and stayed there for the best part of a year, finally rising to number thirty-two, Zappa's highest yet.

In the press release, though, Zappa still talked like a composer: 'The instrumental combinations, the sonority of it is so strange. The way the tunes are voiced out, the violins will either be on the top or bottom of the chord, the clarinet is in the middle, sometimes alternating with the trombone, and the upper edge is usually outlined by a marimba or vibes line. The drums often play the melody along with everybody else. All of this is accompanied by a harmony line or the duplication of the marimba line on a synthesizer. As you can see, there's lots of complicated lines being doubled all over the place – rhythmically and otherwise.' Such points were lost on the rock press, whose post-'68 version of the counterculture was increasingly moralistic and snobbish: a business of condemning low desires in favour of 'progressive' ideals. Once again, outrage at 'sex' songs like 'Camarillo Brillo' and 'Dinah-Moe Humm' obscured musical analysis. Zappa's vibrant new ensemble found few supporters.

For the cover, Zappa re-employed David B. McMacken, the air-brush artist who had designed the *200 Motels* poster and album cover (these were different, since Ringo Starr featured in the film but not on the record). Zappa's instructions were meticulously realised: sitting on the soiled bed, there's roadie Marty Perellis, whose exploits with a fire extinguisher on the Australian tour were legendary; a sexually-abused grapefruit used for 'road relief' by horny tour-drivers; above the bed, there's one of artist Brittinni's syndicated paintings of closed venetian blinds (Zappa was amused to find these in countless Holiday Inns); manager Herbie Cohen emerges through concrete like the tip of a power-drill. Inside the gatefold, Cal Schenkel drew 'TV slime' pooting through the perforations in the hardboard that protected the valves at the back of early-70s TV sets (he also sketched the strangely-protruding 'hold' and 'size' controls).

'I'm The Slime' sets the political agenda, as Zappa excoriated the cultural blight of television. However, he does not stand outside the system he criticises, advising the listener to, say, read more books: on the cover he's portrayed leering from a motel-room TV, while his insights on mass-marketing ('you will do as you are told/until the rights to you are sold') are delivered in the tones of an advertisement voice-over. 'Can't stop the slime, people, lookit me go...' he sings, and his electric guitar, adazzle with effects, seems to exemplify the very process he is decrying.

'Camarillo Brillo' is a portrayal of the sorry state of the US counterculture, the hippie mama who buys her 'alternative' clothing from Sears & Roebuck, the mail-order firm. As allergic as William Burroughs to moralism in any guise, Zappa used sex both as selling-point and accusation. 'She said her stereo was four-way...' refers to Quadrophonic, the latest step beyond stereo that *Overnite Sensation* was originally released in.

'Montana' was written after Zappa glanced at a box of dental floss on the bathroom shelf and decided he needed to write songs that were 'more specific' in terms of his own experience. Its inspired lunacy surfaces in note sequences of bewildering perversion. 'Zirkon-encrusted tweezers', he explained in a radio interview, symbolised 'fake grandeur that might be sexually stimulating'. 'Dinah-Moe Humm' returned to the tweezers, as an (uncredited) Tina Turner and the Ikettes sang ''cause I can't get into it/unless I get out of it'. At Zappa's concerts, this ribald tale became a favourite encore, whole audiences shouting 'Dinah-Moe! Dinah-Moe!' like some monstrous machine. His audience's base desires: the fuel for Zappa's entire project.

'Fifty Fifty' and 'Zomby Woof' featured the extraordinary voice of the late Ricky Lancelotti. 'He auditioned,' Zappa told Rip Rense, 'passed, went home and got ripped, and broke his arm. I said, "Rick, you're not going to make the tour". He used to carry a .45. He had a cassette in which he imitated 100 cartoon voices in 60 seconds. He wanted to get work as a cartoon voice. An old New Jersey tough guy.' Lancelotti's hoarse dementia fuses with Ponty's electric violin and Duke's ripping organ into a hi-tech version of low-down R&B. On stage, 'Dirty Love' was the climax of Zappa's rewrite of Genesis into a parable of poodles, clipping and canine cunnilingus; on record, it was Zappa's jazz-rock version of Iggy Pop's 'Now I Wanna Be Your Dog'. For Zappa, musical complexity did not have to be either juiceless or spiritually pretentious: as post-Miles fusion took off into Scientology and other guru-fixations, a welcome reminder.

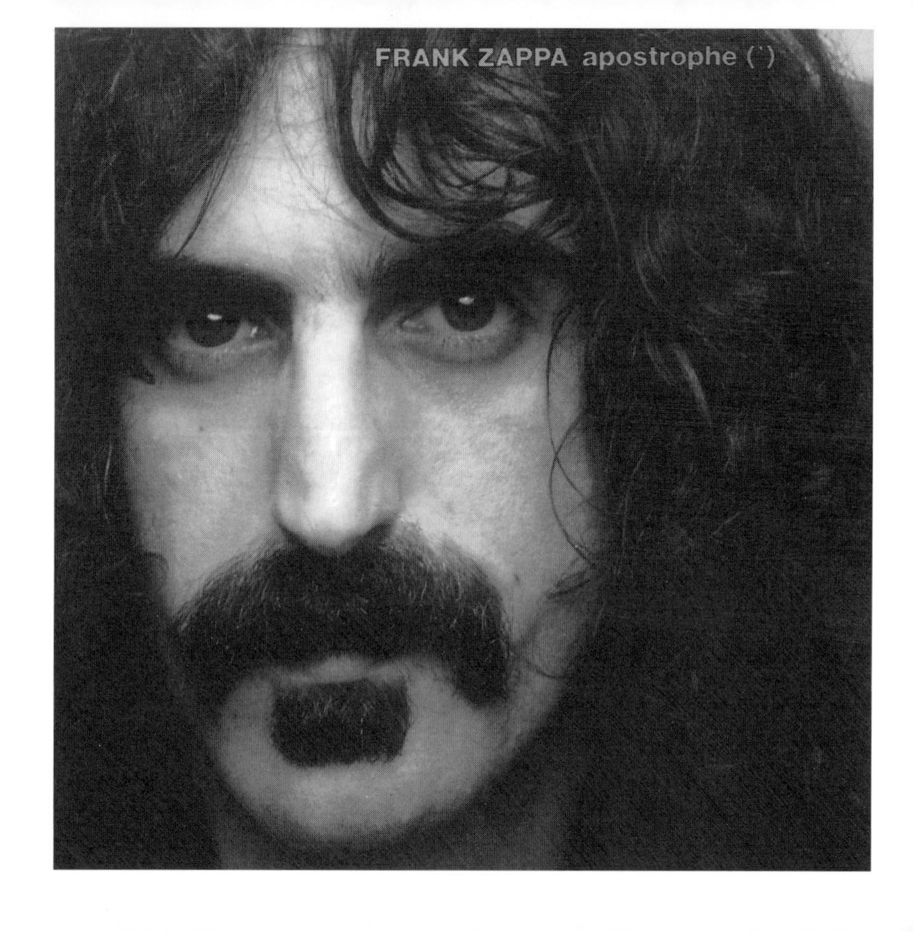
FRANK ZAPPA apostrophe (')

APOSTROPHE (')

(ORIGINAL RELEASE: APRIL 1974; CD RELEASE RYKODISC/RCD 1019)

Zappologist Stuart Lester contends that *Apostrophe (')* is Zappa's most personal, in-focus album: it's therefore appropriate that the cover should consist of a close-up photo-portrait. Recorded at various studios with a wide-ranging personnel over two years, conceptual continuity is dense-packed as musical and verbal details are folded into labyrinthine complexity. It is also one of Zappa's silliest productions, with jokes and ludicrous inventions coming thick and fast, all delivered in an avuncular, facetious manner. Poodles, a theme that arrived with *Over-Nite Sensation*, are much in evidence.

The present writer must own up to one of the more preposterous 'theories' about the record: that it provides a commentary on mortality and the soul, using symbols common to Plato's *Phaedo* and Shakespeare's *King Lear* (see my *Frank Zappa: The Negative Dialectics Of Poodle Play*, pp. 242-251). Not that Zappa consciously used Plato and Shakespeare, merely that these writers played such a formative role in our culture that anyone dealing with heavy themes like existence and non-existence (and what is an apostrophe except a signifier of absence?) will inevitably end up recycling their imagery. Since the *Lear*/*Phaedo* comparisons caused much mirth in reviews, let it be stated that when I declaimed the relevant passage to Zappa in October 1993 (shortly before his death, thus giving my discourse on mortality a certain poignancy), he made no remark – but when I asserted that artists can intuitively touch on themes beyond their conscious ken, Frank nodded vigorously. Certainly, anyone granted Zappa's acquaintance with Zen would question the assumption – universally made by journalists – that a joke could have no bearing on the ultimate profundities.

My only regret is that my own knowledge of European literature at that time was too shallow to inform him that there is also a poodle at the centre of Goethe's *Faust* (the diabolical Mephistopheles first appears to Faust in the form of a giant, shaggy, black poodle). Likewise, I'd not heard bluesman Tampa Red's 'I Want To Play With Your Poodle', where the poodle's 'black curly hair' makes the symbolism distinctly vaginal. When Zappa told *New Musical Express* 'poodles serve as a convenient mechanism for conveying certain philosophical ideas that might otherwise be more difficult', he was talking about their function in his own thought – yet another example of what his wife Gail calls 'prescience'.

From the opening words of 'Don't Eat The Yellow Snow' – 'Dreamed I was an Eskimo...' – Zappa uses the primordial conceit of the dream. Dream-logic allows him to free-associate and make irresponsible connections. Nanook's mother advises him to save his money and resist 'going to the show'. When she tells him to 'watch out where the huskies go/an' don't you eat the yellow snow' the matriarchal advice comes out like an advertising jingle. Nanook resists the baby-seal slaying fur-trapper who was 'strictly from commercial', but Zappa's back-up chorus sings 'strictly commercial' as if they are advertising a car-wash on TV. Awash with puns, reverse-logic and sexual symbolism, Zappa understands advertising as the dream-time of the rational capitalist order, and plunders them for dadaist dysfunctionalism.

'Stink-Foot' may refute *Phaedo*'s thesis about the divine immortality of the soul, but it originated in a TV commercial for foot-spray deodorant (according to Barry Miles' *Visual Documentary*, 'the god (sic!) keels over after the guy takes his shoes off'). 'Excentrifugal Forz' bristles with the subliminal sex-references employed by advertisers. The beturbaned, bejewelled Korla Pandit performed musical exotica on 50s American TV. Here, as 'Korla Plankton' buffs a 'tiny ruby' and his turban straightens up to 'eject a little ooze', genital excitements infuse the imagery.

'Cosmik Debris' and 'Uncle Remus' dealt with less intimate concerns. The first was a satire on Maharaj Ji, a child guru recruiting psychic casualties from the drug culture; the second questioned the relative quiescence of the movement for Black emancipation. 'Uncle Remus' is a gentle reprimand, noting how protest was being abandoned for fashion: the ''Fro' is an Afro, the natural-look hair-do; water from riot-police hoses could harm your 'sharp' clothes. The 'little jockeys' refers to the statuettes of black stable-boys in Hollywood gardens, targets for anti-racist vandals. Co-written with George Duke, the song is replete with his characteristic chordal lyricism and warm funk.

On 'Nanook Rubs It', Zappa predicted that 'the circular motion' would 'take the place of the mud shark in your mythology' (*Fillmore East* was as big a hit in Australia as *Hot Rats* in Britain; during his 1973 tour, Zappa noted that the Mud Shark dance had indeed gone global). *Lumpy Gravy*'s 'round things are boring' has turned into something altogether less disdainful; as Zappa proceeds with the injunction 'rub it!', sinister voices may be heard intoning 'here Fido... here Fido'. As Zappa abused stuffed poodles on stage and made dark references to audience 'stupidity', he seemed to be finding something craven and poodle-like about the crowds who flocked to see him.

Apostrophe (') shot into the top ten. Zappa even released a 7" single from it (a version of 'Don't Eat The Yellow Snow' which a DJ had edited down for airplay). However, Zappa's relationship to commercial success remained problematic, fraught with innuendo, satire and sarcasm – and biz-defying efforts to perpetrate musical grotesques woefully lacking in the all-important 'commercial potential'.

ZAPPA / MOTHERS
ROXY & ELSEWHERE

ROXY & ELSEWHERE

(ORIGINAL RELEASE: SEPTEMBER 1974;
CD RELEASE RYKODISC/RCD 1020)

Before the advent of the 80-minute CD, the vinyl 'live double album' was the usual means for touring bands to document their shows. Uniquely, Zappa used the form to present new material (his habit of road-testing songs before release led to him being – after Bob Dylan – the most bootlegged act in rock). Now a convenient single CD, *Roxy & Elsewhere* was originally two 12" records: the original tracklisting included 'preambles' at the start of each side. These gave Uncle Frank a chance to inform audiences about extra-terrestrial gratification, small-town nostalgia, monster movies and the dubious state of jazz.

The *Roxy & Elsewhere* band was a yeasty combination of spontaneity and discipline, with a rich sound helped by Kerry McNabb's brilliant engineering. The addition of drummer Chester Thompson added funky impetus. The video *Dub Room Special* shows the sheer fun the players had in this band: percussionist Ruth Underwood emerged as a star, her evident delight at Zappa's perverse metrics expressed in a beaming smile and a performance that was practically a continual dance.

If Zappa-fans are called upon to demonstrate his particular virtues, they can do no better than to compare his ode to sadomasochism, 'Penguin In Bondage', to 'Venus In Furs' by The Velvet Underground. Lou Reed lists predictable clichés, while Zappa conjures up a hitherto-unattested scenario reeking with bizarre proclivities and still-more-bizarre phobias. 'Havin' her jumpin' through a hoopa real fire/with some Kleenex wrapped around a coat-hang wire' might derive from a stunt Flo & Eddie performed with 'Little Carl' (a small inflatable penguin), but it also said something about the surreal nature of the sex act. Singer Napoleon Murphy Brock was discovered by Zappa singing in a bar in Hawaii (Zappa was impressed that he said he couldn't join The Mothers until completing his booking). Brock's infectious humour and vocal gymnastics permeate *Roxy*, his repartee with George Duke providing perfect specimens of 70s soul-bro' jive.

'Echidna's Arf', 'Don't You Ever Wash That Thing?' and 'Be-Bop Tango' were deliberately 'difficult' compositions, challenges tackled with glee by this ensemble. Whereas contemporary jazz rock's aspirations to complexity tended to downplay its funky roots – and result in etiolated, neo-classical twiddles – Tom Fowler's bass and George Duke's keyboards kept everything sassy and greasy. 'Son Of Orange County' reprised 'Oh No' from *Weasels*; Zappa's aside 'I am not a crook' was a famous live-on-TV plea by an increasingly besieged President Nixon. It made the song a political jibe, though less explicit than the contemporaneous 'Dickie's Such An Asshole' (see *You Can't Do That On Stage Anymore Vol.3*). Zappa remarked that with a musician like Duke comping, you couldn't help sounding good; his guitar solo on 'Trouble Every Day' is gorgeous.

Roxy finishes in chaos as audience members were invited to dance to Duke's scat vocals. This 'self-indulgence' offended critics, but Zappa's openness to accident and event was the necessary condiment to the rigour of his charts. Indubitably, *Roxy* was packed with more musical ideas than most 'live double' releases of the 70s. When it first appeared on CD – on Zappa's own label – he added a message: 'Sometimes you can be surprised that "The universe works whether or not you understand it"'. Zappa's manifesto of Zen materialism was omitted from the Rykodisc release.

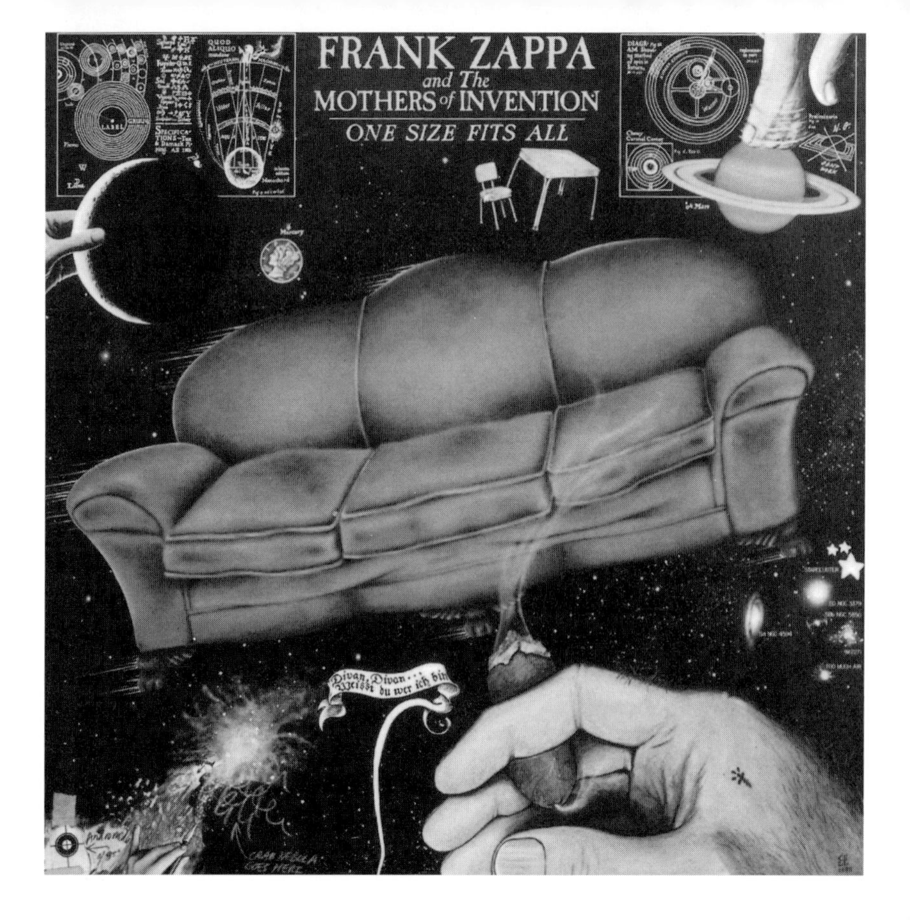

FRANK ZAPPA
and The
MOTHERS of INVENTION
ONE SIZE FITS ALL
Divan, Divan...
Weisst du wer ich bin

ONE SIZE FITS ALL

(ORIGINAL RELEASE: JUNE 1975; CD RELEASE RYKODISC/RCD 1021)

Although hardcore fans are loath to name favourite albums – some even insisting that it's the ones that rub you up the wrong way that reveal the greatest treasures (eventually) – *One Size Fits All* regularly wins readers' polls in the T'Mershi Duween fanzine. The band was the same as *Roxy*, except that Ralph Humphrey had gone, Johnny 'Guitar' Watson sings some choruses and Captain Beefheart plays harp (for contractual purposes billed as 'Bloodshot Rollin' Red'). Described by Charles Shaar Murray in *New Musical Express* as 'funk riffs and heavy metal textures... whimsical little songs with little appreciable idea content and a tetch of elementary word play', *One Size Fits All* was as elastic in its semantics as its title. Some believe it is Zappa's most consummate cosmo-materialist statement, a hi-tech extrusion of traditions as ancient as Pythagoras, Theodore de Bry and the Kaballah.

The cover illustrated a blasphemous scenario that originated with the Flo & Eddie edition of The Mothers, 'Geff Mij Wat Vloer Bedekking Onder Dezer Vette Zwevende Sofa', in which God attempted to make a home movie involving His girlfriend and Squat the Magic Pig (see 'Once Upon A Time' on *You Can't Do That On Stage Anymore Vol. 1*). We are looking from God's point of view, a cigar grasped in His/Our hand (which is tattooed with a 'Pachuco cross', like Ruben's on the cover of *Ruben & the Jets*). On the left of the title Cal Schenkel placed a parody of a Theodore de Bry etching from a Robert Fludd compendium on mysticism (it graced the cover of Harry Smith's 1952 *Anthology Of American Folk*, a collection that provided Bob Dylan with a substantial amount of early inspiration). It shows God's hand tuning the 'Celestial Monochord'. In Schenkel's version, the alchemical diagram has become phonographic: the realms of harmony beneath the 'mysterium magnum' are listed as mono, stereo and quodrophonic. The planetary system to the left has a label, 'gruuvs' and a hole. On the other side, a clockwork-universe account of the method of spin in Saturn lists three spheres: 'sodium and sulpher', 'scotch and sodium' and 'sodium and gommorah', plus a 'chewy caramel centre'. New stars – too small to read in the Zappa Records CD-issue, but legible in the Rykodisc fold-out – are named for Zappa's cat Gorgo and dog Dogess. 'KNARF (uview)' reverses 'Frank' to find 'Arf'; another star celebrates the (posthumous) naming of an asteroid '(3834)Zappafrank'. Domestic and cosmic names are punned together. Zappa was convinced that the divine and the human were not of different stuff (the moral of much of his – and Schenkel's – 'humour').

'Inca Roads' took its storyline from Von Daniken's 70s best-seller *Was God An Astronaut?*. The deep, funky bass, assymmetrical time-signature and Duke's falsetto give it an eerie resemblance to Yes. Cosmic speculation is reduced to infantile fun-and-games and references to Chester Thompson's appearances in a gorilla suit; lines about 'booger bears' derived from jive nursery-tales George Duke would recite while accompanying himself on finger-cymbals. Spoken-word interludes that are meant to portray regular-citizen amazement at UFOs include the words 'why don't you sharpen it, then?', This phrase derived from one of the builders working on Zappa's (ever-growing) house (he'd talk to himself while working out solutions to, say, a blunt chisel). Arcane personal references would enter band-lore and end up in the oddest places.

'Can't Afford No Shoes' dealt with the economic slump, while 'Pojama People' was Zappa's song against academic musicians and their finicky ways, though the details of the pyjamas they wear – flannel, with 'trap-doors' to allow defecation – stem from Zappa's own childhood memories. The song is guitar-driven, with Duke's chords and Thompson's drums flailing about loosely, as if Zappa is also including a swipe at rock bands that think that a 'jam' is as good as a worked-out composition. As usual, no-one gets off the hook.

'Florentine Pogen' is named after a biscuit; Zappa called it a 'love song'. 'Color-note organ' seems to refer to Scriabin and his synaesthetic equations between notes and colours; the harmonic atmosphere is redolent of 'Penguin In Bondage'. The lyrics disintegrate into personal association and wordplay ('hratche-plche' was the transcription of city-hall straights drooling after office girls in 'Brown Shoes Don't Make It', as printed in the 1967 *International Times*, though omitted from the Rykodisc lyric sheet with *Absolutely Free*). However, the musical logic is cogent as Zappa revels in the contrasting depths Kerry McNabb's recording equipment at Paramount Studios made available. The same fascination structures 'Andy', which contrasts singers Duke and Watson in an interrogation of what creates the illusion of 'depth' in music – and people. 'Evelyn, A Modified Dog' continued Zappa's mystico-materialist musings on the nature of musical resonance, hinting that music is a message from a sphere humans can barely comprehend, while also mocking the bourgeois accoutrements – doilies, pianos, curtains – of 'classical' culture.

'San Ber'dino', like 'Can't Afford No Shoes', is 'straightahead rock'n'roll', though in this context it sounds abstract and strange. It makes sinister parallels between the limited horizons of married life and penal incarceration. The album title's initials – OSFA – are an anagram of 'sofa': hence 'Sofa No 2' is the rousing finale, being the song God sings to His sofa. German lyrics give it a suitably Wagnerian afflatus. Zappa's poetic, imagistic links between domesticity and cosmos keep returning to the claustrophobic banality of everyday life under capitalism. As he said at the time, sounding like sci-fi writer Philip K. Dick: 'when the illusion of freedom becomes too expensive to maintain, they will just take down the scenery, pull back the curtains, and you will see the brick wall at the back of the theatre'.

BONGO FURY

(ORIGINAL RELEASE: OCTOBER 1975;
CD RELEASE RYKODISC/RCD 1022)

By using live tracks as the basis for studio productions, Zappa transcended the distinction between 'live' and 'studio' recording. *Bongo Fury* was ostensibly live at the Armadillo in Texas – a venue name-checked in 'Inca Roads' on *One Size*, and celebrated for a blues vibe – but included 'Selected Studio Wonderment' too. Virgin contract in tatters, Captain Beefheart came out from behind his Bloodshot alias and is pictured on the cover under a wide-brimmed hat. Wakefield-based Zappologist Kitty Reese has pointed out that Beefheart's shoes-without-socks recalls Albert Einstein, appropriate given the vertigo induced by his two poems: details recorded with such surreal intensity they explode subject/object detachment. In an interview, talking about slide-guitarist Denny Walley and Beefheart's Howlin'-Wolf-type growl, Zappa admitted he was 'moving towards a blues thing'. Combined with the cover photo – a snapshot in a grim diner – the guitar-heavy, scrambled music was a retort to the self-congratulation of the American Bicenntenial: 'opaque melodies that would bug most people, music from the other side of the fence' as Beefheart had it on 'Sam With The Showing Scalp Flat Top'.

'Debra Kadabra' is a descendant of 'Camarillo Brillo'. Beefheart sounds desperate as he recites Zappa's words, an avalanche of subcultural debris, his pronunciation startlingly mimetic (his description of shoes being 'too tight' sounds tight to the point of asphyxiation). Instrumental effects buffet him as if he's a performing bear; when he says 'give me bas relief' and a regular bass-line starts up, the listener feels relieved too. 'Carolina Hard-Core Ecstasy' is a tale of groupie masochism, an extension of 'why don't you treat me mean?' on 'St Alphonzo's Pancake Breakfast' on *Apostrophe(')*. However, the narrator is wearing a 'Roger Daltrey' cape; this rockist 'stomping' is riven with sarcasm.

'Poofter's Froth, Wyoming' (a genuine address) describes small-town America cashing in on the Bicenntenial and its souvenir trash, oblivious of the fact that 'two hundred years have gone kaput!' (Beefheart pronounces the German word for 'broken' with the emphasis on 'poot', Zappa's slang for flatulence.)'Cucamonga', like *Roxy*'s 'Village Of The Sun', was nostalgic, this time about Studio Z and the early 60s: the days and nights Beefheart and Zappa spent cutting sides with Ray Collins and Motorhead Sherwood.

'Advance Romance' is a scripted jam, Zappa's freakish style contrasting with Denny Walley's slide-blues prowess. Potato-head Bobby (first referenced on 'San Ber'dino' on *One Size*) has his fry 'frenched' by a scheming devil of a woman. Mention of food-stamp queues brings in a chill air of realism. Beefheart's 'Man With The Woman Head' is a close-up of Hollywood squalor, surreal grotesques squeezed from the mundane. 'Muffin Man' – a favourite encore – was a negative polemic with a gloriously lyrical, eruptive guitar solo from Zappa.

When he wishes goodnight to Austin Texas 'wherever you are', you feel Zappa and Beefheart have successfully brought the pain and glory of the blues to record buyers wherever they might be. Often dismissed as inferior to their previous collaboration, *Trout Mask Replica* (but then what record isn't?), *Bongo Fury*'s blues has a special place in Zappa's oeuvre.

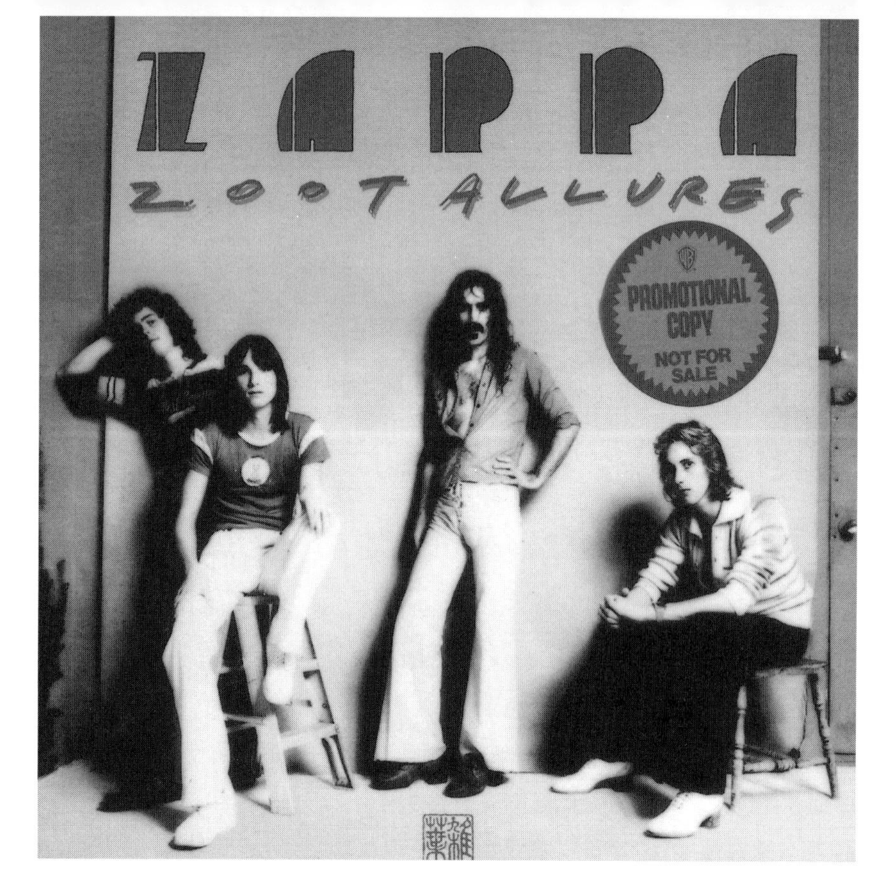
ZAPPA
ZOOT ALLURES
PROMOTIONAL
COPY
NOT FOR
SALE

WARNER BROTHERS VERSUS CATHER

ZOOT ALLURES

(ORIGINAL RELEASE: OCTOBER 1976;
CD RELEASE RYKODISC/RCD 10523)

For the cover of *Zoot Allures*, Zappa posed in unrepentant, fuck-off-to-punk flares. However, as if acknowledging the punk threat looming on the horizon – this was the year the Ramones, the Pistols and the Clash were vowing to kill off rock 'dinosaurs' – he did surround himself with youth. A pudgy Patrick O'Hearn leans against the studio wall, while a fresh-faced Eddie Jobson looked on nervously, seated on a stool. They were members of Zappa's band that toured between October 1976 and March 1977, but neither play on the record! Seated on a step-ladder, drummer Terry Bozzio – Zappa's chief musical collaborator – looked still more boyish. Appropriately, the logo on his T-shirt read 'Angels' (a baseball team). Surrounded by all this cherubic innocence, Zappa looked dangerously swarthy and demonic (his trousers have an enormous bulge at the crotch). On the reverse (cropped in the Rykodisc CD booklet), the others hold still while Zappa does a stupid knee-bend, as if mocking the whole charade. A Japanese transliteration of Zappa's name appears on both sides.

The cover design of *Zoot Allures* was by Cal Schenkel, the photographs by Gary Heery, who had taken photos for *Good Singin' Good Playin'* by Grand Funk Railroad, an album Zappa produced at this time. One of the engineers for the vocals on that record, Davey Moire, sang lead on the opener, 'Wind Up Workin' In A Gas Station'. This frenzied song about dead-end jobs was a punk parody, though Terry Bozzio's explosive polyrhythms were far from primitive.

'Black Napkins', named to commemorate the tableware at a promoter's thanksgiving dinner in Japan, was recorded at the Kosei Nenkin Kaikan in Osaka on 3 February 1976. It is the sole realtime performance on the record. Zappa's soaring, Santana-like guitar is the perfect tense intro to the lascivious echo-chamber that is 'The Torture Never Stops'. An audio snuff-movie, this was the soundtrack to Zappa's cover hard-on, and leads to 'Ms Pinky', an ode to a sex aid shaped like a child's head with an open mouth and built-in vibrators (the full explanation may be heard on 'Lonely Person Devices' on *You Can't Do That On Stage Anymore Vol.6*). Zappa might tease the listener with audio-porn, but he isn't concerned to cover up the lonely pleasures it invites.

Like *Bongo Fury*, side two of *Zoot Allures* begins with sly, suggestive R&B aerated by Beefheart's bluesy harmonica. 'Find Her Finer' is cynical advice about approaches to women: 'don't let her know you are smart, the universe is nowhere to start'. Like the rest of the album, bass sound and pace are sleazy and reverberating. 'Friendly Little Finger' was recorded using 'experimental re-synchronization', which meant combining tracks recorded at different times and by musicians who weren't listening to each other. Montage like this is a technique familiar in cinema. Though used in Hip-Hop and Ambient today, in 1976 it was rare in music. Back then, multitracking was a means of achieving a 'perfect' real-group emulation, not a tool for 'experiment': Zappa had to fight his engineers to do it. Zappa used the technique extensively on *Joe's Garage*, when he called it 'xenochrony' (alien time) floating his guitar solos over rhythm tracks that aren't playing in the same time-zone.

A snatch from the hymn 'Bringing In The Sheaves' introduces 'Wonderful Wino', a song originally recorded on Jeff Simmons' *Lucille Has Messed My Mind Up. Again*, a song of sleaze and filth customized to offend the 'clean-cut folks'. The title track of 'Zoot Allures' is astonishing; guitar, string harp and marimba are recorded with extraordinary resonance. Although devoid of lyrics, everything is coloured by the atmosphere of the preceding songs. 'Disco Boy' satirised disco, but sounds more like Glam Rock. 'You never go doody, that's what you think,' leered Zappa, 'leave his hair alone, but you can kiss his comb'. As usual, good looks and sartorial cool are denounced as lack of sensuous engagement and concession to peer pressure. Zappa details the misery of a failed sexual encounter, and recommends masturbation. Throughout the record, Zappa had quite literally – via overdubbing – been 'playing with himself': 'Disco Boy' is as much a cry of pain about the composer's solitude and alienation as it is satire of teen frustration (the Rykodisc release credits a 'Sharkie Barker' for background vocals on this track, rather than the original's Sparkie Parker; even personnel details have been warped by anxieties about vagina dentata and woofing canines).

Beneath their trademark 'green-tinted' disc-holder, Rykodisc included one of Cal Schenkel's graphics from Zappa's 1980 world-tour programme: it shows sex aids and hardcore porn images rendered strange and abstract by misaligned lithography. *Zoot Allures* works the same way: experimental re-synchronisation of exploitative song-forms result in unheard strangenesses.

ZAPPA IN NEW YORK

(ORIGINAL RELEASE: MARCH 1978;
CD RELEASE RYKODISC/RCD 10524/25)

Zappa In New York was the fruit of compromise. According to Gail Zappa, Zappa originally conceived a four-record box-set to be called *Läther*. Warner Brothers wouldn't release such an expensive item, so he 'reluctantly reformatted it' as four separate releases – *Zappa In New York*, *Studio Tan*, *Sleep Dirt* and *Orchestral Favorites* – and redelivered them. 'Nothing like this had ever happened before. No artist had cured his obligations by delivering all the albums required at once. They wouldn't pay him. They wouldn't release him.' So, in revenge, Zappa broadcast the original two-and-a-half-hour *Läther* over the radio, telling listeners to tape it off the air (although according to Paul Rambali – NME 28 January 1978 – Zappa created *Läther* by 're-editing' the four rejected albums; Simon Prentis's note on Rykodisc's posthumous release of *Läther* is non-committal).

One thing is clear: *Läther* is a bone fide masterpiece, a staggering fold-in of all Zappa's styles – rock songs, orchestral interludes, chamber jazz, electric guitar – all segued bewteen snippets of spoken word and effects in the manner of *We're Only In It For The Money*. Zappa's 'reluctant' reformatting created albums of greater generic coherence, but without the contrasts and scope of *Läther*.

Curiously, once Zappa had secured rights to his master-tapes in the late-70s, he reissued them in the form Warner Brothers had used, even retaining graphics he had no part in commissioning. Perhaps he felt it would be wrong to 'rewrite history' and that his oeuvre should comprise his records as actually released. Now, with the posthumous release of *Läther*, buyers can choose how they want to hear the music.

Of the four albums delivered to Warners, *Zappa In New York* was the only one with cover and sleevenotes supplied by Zappa. The CD-issue has five additions, making it a two-disc release: 'Punky's Whips' (originally omitted by Warners in case Punky Meadows, the target of Zappa's satire, waxed litigious – though some pressings in England had the track), 'Cruisin' For Burgers', 'Pound For A Brown', 'I'm The Slime' and 'The Torture Never Stops'.

Zappa In New York opens with 'Titties & Beer', a reductionist account of male priorities that invariably causes indignation. It was an opportunity to goad drummer Terry Bozzio, who had to wear a rubber mask and play the part of the devil. In the version Zappa chose for release, their improvised dialogue includes: Zappa – 'I'm only interested in two things. See if you can guess what they are.' Bozzio – 'Let's see now, maybe Stravinsky and...'. Bozzio had a point.

In 1972 Zappa had played the devil in a performance of Stravinsky's *Soldier's Tale* at the Hollywood Bowl: 'Titties & Beer' is a rewrite of the story. In Stravinsky's original, the soldier's soul is represented by a violin. Zappa's exclamation 'Up Jumped the Devil!' refers to an obscure tune recorded by violinist Stuff Smith (in 'late 1949 or early 1950' according to Stuffologist Anthony Barnett). 'Don't they pay you well for the stuff that you do?' he asks Bozzio. Just as Zappa's violinists (Sugarcane Harris, Jean-Luc Ponty, Eddie Jobson, L. Shankar, Ashley Arbuckle) leapt the classical/blues score/improvisation divide, so the devilry of 'Titties & Beer' conflates Igor Stravisnky and Stuff Smith.

'Cruisin' For Burgers' transformed *Uncle Meat*'s dreamy nostalgia for teenage pleasures into a thunderous workout, each instrument pursuing a different rhythm. 'I Promise Not To Come In Your Mouth' was *Läther*'s title-track, with a tingling Moog solo by Eddie Jobson. 'Punky's Whips' is one of Zappa's most magical creations; Terry Bozzio's homoerotic impulses are depicted with great subtlety. Electric guitar, horns and percussion combine in a totally original manner. Opera, but not as we know it, Giuseppe.

'Honey, Don't You Want A Man Like Me?' is finely-observed satire on mating-game rituals. In later performances, office-girl Betty's favourite group changed from Helen Reddy – famous for the feminist anthem 'I Am Woman' (1972) – to Twisted Sister, a cartoon heavy-metal outfit (Zappa's repartee to a heckler – 'fuck you, Zappa!'/'and fuck you, too, buddy, fuck you very much!' – was cut from *In New York*, but appeared on *Läther*).

'The Legend Of The Illinois Enema Bandit' took off from a true-life court-case, developing into an epic of anal-sadism as Zappa vented scatological fury against college-educated women. The scabrous, stinky suggestiveness of his guitar solo – positively reeking with coprophilic drives – illustrates the aesthetic advantages of using dubious subject-matter. 'I'm The Slime' is a splendid, brass-driven arrangement of the song from *Over-Nite Sensation*, introduced by TV-presenter Don Pardo. 'Pound For A Brown' became a concert stand-by over the years; whereas the original Mothers pondered over its assymetrical time signature, later bands found it a convenient testing-ground for instrumental aromas.

'Manx Needs Women' and a new arrangement of *One Size Fits All*'s 'Sofa' are magnificent deployments of amplified forces. 'Black Page' presented musical difficulty as a crowd-pleasing stunt, stripping off its trappings of class and sophistication. 'The Purple Lagoon' – the 'music music' fourth side of *In New York*'s original vinyl – had guests the Brecker brothers and Ronnie Cuber play jazz solos over a rhythmic minefield. On *Zappa In New York*, rock power, jazz chops and classical organisation achieved an expressive pungency 70s Fusion was hard put to emulate.

STUDIO TAN

(ORIGINAL RELEASE: SEPTEMBER 1978;C
D RELEASE RYKODISC/RCD 10524/25)

Studio Tan presented two sides of the eight-sided box-set *Läther*. The twenty minute 'The Adventures Of Greggary Peccary' was side eight, one of those epic productions with which Zappa liked to close a major work. For listeners repelled by Zappa's vocal delivery – those who prefer *Hot Rats* to, say, *Apostrophe(')* – this album cannot be recommended: 'Greggary Peccary' is basically Zappa narrating a cartoon-style story aided by a thousand-and-one musical jokes and sound effects. In the 90s, the music Raymond Scott and Carl Stalling wrote for cartoons is widely celebrated; in the 1970s, Zappa's penchant for high-speed triviality bucked convention. As in 'Billy The Mountain' on *Just Another Band From LA*, Zappa tells his story via a series of clichés that instantly trigger visual images (eg 'acid burnt-out eyeballs' or 'they park their cars in a pseudo-waggon-train formation'). However, this is not a raucous band ad-libbing on stage, but a meticulously-crafted, multi-tracked wonder.

The Rykodisc edition credits a small band: George Duke, the Fowler brothers and Chester Thompson: strings, woodwinds, saxophone, orchestral chimes, marimba, xylophone all go uncredited. The fast flow of ideas is dazzling and could sustain pages of analysis. To take one example, the motif played after the words 'flower power' is the 'mongoloid folk-rock riff' Zappa deliberately built into 'Tryin' To Grow A Chin' (a *Läther* song that first appeared on *Sheik Yerbouti*). According to Zappa's doctrine that linear time is an illusion, Greggary Peccary 'invents' the calendar, thus giving people the chance to find out how old they are. 'What hath God wrought?' asks a voice, quoting the first words ever mechanically reproduced (Thomas Edison's; *Läther*'s original cover pastiched the label on the sound cylinders manufactured at 'Edison Laboratories'). For Zappa, our experience of time is dependent on technologies of record and replay: memory is a historical product. However, despite such deep thoughts (all delivered at the frantic pace of a Tom & Jerry short), Zappa remains cynical about the motives of 'philostophers' in explaining the world: whatever you ask, they'll 'see that you pay'. Truth is a social conundrum, to be discovered in resistance to rip-offs and economic exploitation rather than in crediting pundits.

'Revised Music For Guitar And Low-Budget Orchestra' is a glossy remake of the suite Zappa wrote for Jean-Luc Ponty's *King Kong*. 'Lemme Take You To The Beach' is parodic surf pop with Grand Funk Railroad engineer Davey Moire on falsetto, Don Brewer on bongos and Eddie Jobson 'yodelling'. 'RDNZL' is a mighty tune, glistening with bogus pomp. Its different sections stroke the passage of time in opposite directions, suggesting that the uniformity of clock time is not the whole story. Zappa's solo has vim and lyricism, George Duke's fulminous piano bouncing him up to ever-renewed heights.

The striking cover was by Gary Panter of *Raw Comix*, the first of three commissioned by Warner Brothers for the albums Zappa had delivered without artwork. It shows someone in a deck chair sweating under studio lights. When Rykodisc came to issue *Studio Tan*, *Sleep Dirt* and *Orchestral Favorites* in 1995, they got back in touch with Panter. He provided extra sketches to appear beneath the transparent inlay-tray in each.

SLEEP DIRT

(ORIGINAL RELEASE: JANUARY 1979;
CD RELEASE RYKODISC/RCD 10527)

Sleep Dirt is a collection of the less definable music from *Läther*, together with two extras: the title track, and 'Time Is Money' (Rykodisc now include the latter as an 'extra' on the 3CD issue of *Läther*). There's a lot of guitar, both acoustic and virtual-arena electric, but it's not rock. There's a lot of George Duke's piano, but it's not jazz. There's a lot of score-playing, but it's not classical. How to define it? Weird, certainly.

Originally, none of the tunes had lyrics, but when it came to CD-release, Zappa recorded soprano Thana Harris on 'Flambay', 'Spider Of Destiny' and 'Time Is Money' (all songs from Zappa's never-to-be musical *Hunchentoot*). Her strident, off-Broadway renditions disappointed fans of the original *Sleep Dirt*, so now the vinyl release is highly prized (though all three appear without the vocal overdub on *Läther*). Harris's singing makes the music less remarkable. This is a pity, because the combination of jazz piano, staggered drums and rippling vibes is quite unprecedented.

'Filthy Habits' is one of Zappa's strongest forays into guitar diabolism, an irresistible surge of overdubbage and feedback. Barbaric, visceral splendours to make the blood boil. 'Time Is Money' used studio-feedback for Zappa's guitar and intimately-recorded bass from Patrick O'Hearn, perpetrating something altogether weird. 'Regyptian Strut' overdubbed Bruce Fowler's trombone, creating the kind of Hollywood 'epic' fraudulence Zappa joked about on *The Grand Wazoo*. 'Sleep Dirt' is an acoustic guitar duet between Zappa and James 'Bird Legs' Youman (who replaced Tom Fowler on *One Size Fits All* when the latter broke his hand), Zappa making silvery, lyrical assertions over Youman's ostinato. 'The Ocean Is The Ultimate Solution' – originally named 'One More Time For The World' (a quote from 'Tryin' To Grow A Chin') – proposes a new kind of studio music, where loud arena-feedback guitar can play over intimate bass and drums. The rhythmic flurries and disjunctures of Zappa's orchestral composition are here realised through a different method – via musicians capable of the rhythmic push of rock and jazz. Like 'Canard Du Jour' on *Shut Up 'N' Play Yer Guitar*, this is the sound of Zappa in his home studio, achieving seriously evocative music with his favourite musicians.

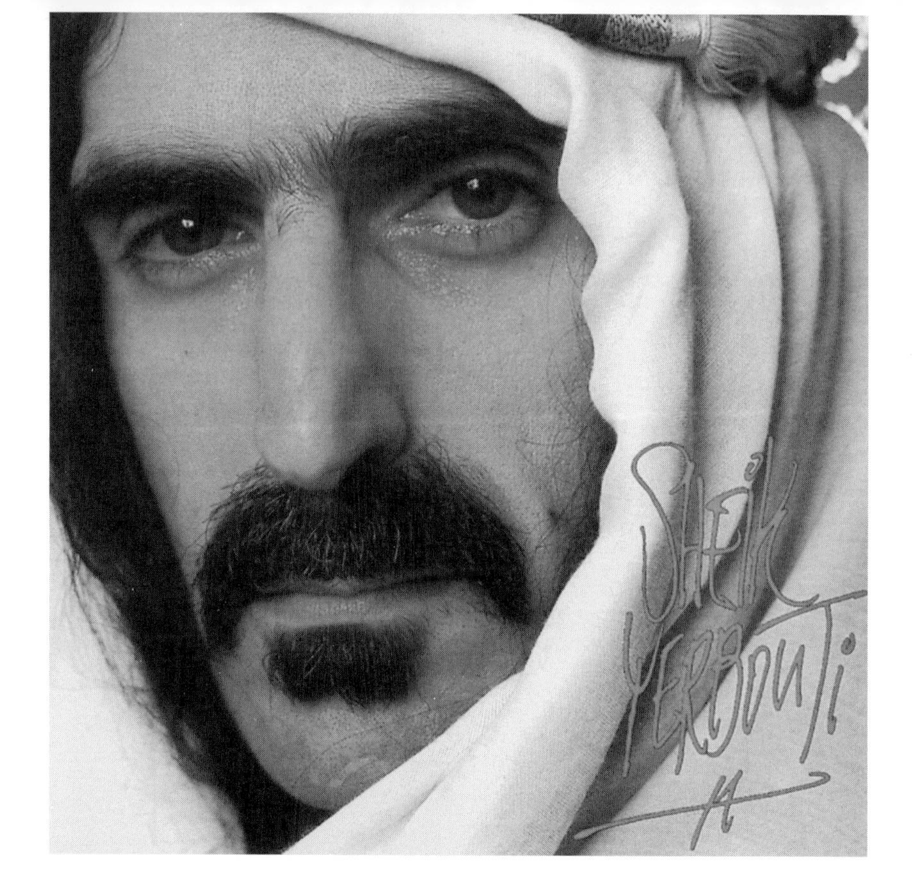
Sheik
Yerbouti

SHEIK YERBOUTI

(ORIGINAL RELEASE: MARCH 1979;
CD RELEASE RYKODISC/RCD 10528)

Sheik Yerbouti stands with *Them Or Us* as one of Zappa's epic rock records. The title punned on K.C. And The Sunshine Band's 1976 hit 'Shake Your Booty'; Zappa's on-cover Bedouin tarboosh emphasized his Sheik-of-Araby physiognomy. 'I Have Been In You' was a ribald rejoinder to Peter Frampton's top-selling 'I'm In You', but it was also a stunning example of a state-of-the-art, three-dimensional studio-mix, with swooping choruses and an insinuating, close-miked vocal. The music is organised like cabaret, with different band members stepping forward to display their talents. On 'Flakes' for example, Adrian Belew (a guitarist Zappa had discovered doing Roy Orbison imitations in a Nashville bar) is unleashed on a Bob Dylan routine. Onstage, Belew had a crewcut and a grey jumpsuit with a label reading 'Lt Punk': he brought a manic violence to Zappa's music.

'Broken Hearts Are For Assholes' detailed the homoerotic implications of the leather concept, as well as the delights of heterosexual sodomy: 'don't fool yourself, girl, I'm gonna ram it up your poop chute' was sung to a dinky pseudo-reggae beat, giving it a surreal charm to those aware of Bob Marley and Burning Spear. 'I'm So Cute' was a 'punk' freak-out by drummer Terry Bozzio intercut with sped-up munchkin vocals listing his dietary fetishes (before Black Flag, ginseng root and vitamin Bs making you cool and cute was about as close Californians could get to the punk ethic). Mothers fans like Charles Shaar Murray and Savage Pencil, now in the thick of punk, were aghast: how could Zappa be so wrong, so misinformed? When Bozzio split to form a 'New Wave' band called Missing Persons, it was clear that Zappa's satire was as prescient as ever; just that his listening post was Hollywood Boulevard rather than the Kings Road.

'Jones Crusher' set images of male

sexual panic to hi-speed rock'n'roll; 'What Ever Happened To All The Fun In The World' and 'We've Got To Get Into Something Real' were spoken-word/effects collages from *Läther*: intimate, angstvoll backstage chat that make the arena rock fury around them still more shockingly loud and public. 'Rat Tomago' was a guitar feature sliced from a live version of 'The Torture Never Stops' from Berlin.

'Bobby Brown', later a top-ten hit in Norway and a biggie in German discos, was a locker-room ditty that swiped at every kind of sexual option – set to a sumptuous melody. 'Rubber Shirt' was more 'experimental re-synchronisation' (a technique debuted on *Zoot Allures*), a showcase for Patrick O'Hearn's oily fretless bass. 'The Sheik Yerbouti Tango' is appropriately camp, the perfect soundtrack to Zappa's flamboyant cover pose.

'Tryin' To Grow A Chin' was suicidal teenage angst, Terry Bozzio wound up to a pitch of frenzy. In the same way that 'Bobby Brown' aligned degraded lyrics to incongrously beautiful music, 'City Of Tiny Lites' – another feature for Belew – coupled micro-hallucinations of domestic squalor to a soaring melody. Led Zeppelin would have had words about meadows and stars: as usual, Zappa is determined to show that immediate reality is more bizarre and fascinating than the romantic sublime.

'Jewish Princess' got Zappa in trouble with the Anti-Defamation League. He rebutted charges of anti-semitism by writing an equally offensive song about his own racial type – 'Catholic Girls' (see *Joe's Garage*). However, given his photo-portrait on the cover, it seems that Zappa is not so much denigrating 'another' race as expressing preference for oriental sensuousness versus white-bread anaemia. You can chop these arguments around all day, but in terms of aesthetics, when Zappa describes 'a garlic aroma that could level Tacoma' he is describing the pungency of his own art rather than making an accusation from a position of puritan cleanliness (he and Steve Vai had an expression, 'put garlic in your playing', which meant using non-standard harmonies). Certainly, the way the song is introduced – pick-up phrases recalling the crowd scene in 'America Drinks' on *Absolutely Free* – shows that Zappa thinks racial characterisations are as dumb as astrology.

'Wild Love' is reminscent of Steely Dan, though the trademark marimbas doubling the melody line – a technique Zappa learned from Charles Ives – make it Zappaesque too. According to Adrian Belew, the lyrics for 'Yo' Mama' were written as admonishment after he hadn't learned the whole of 'Little House I Used To Live In' for a rehearsal. The 'some town outside' Nurnberg guitar solo – dropped in over an alien backing track and buttressed by extensive keyboard overdubbage courtesy Tommy Mars – is one of Zappa's most extreme statements. The playing bursts out of linear sanity into a torrid warzone of distortion and sonic event.

FRANK ZAPPA

ORCHESTRAL

FAVORITES

ORCHESTRAL FAVORITES

(ORIGINAL RELEASE: MAY 1979; CD RELEASE RYKODISC/RCD 10529)

Simon Prentis argues that 'lumped all together, the *Orchestral Favorites* album can sometimes feel too heavy to be fully accessible', and says he prefers to hear the orchestral tracks segued amongst amongst the songs and spoken-word of *Läther*. The album was recorded at UCLA's Royce Hall on 17 and 18 September 1975, with a 37-piece orchestra conducted by Michael Zearott. Zappa achieved a muscular and forthright sound by using close-up mics and a multi-track (instead of the pair of 'crossed-mics' favoured by classical purists), and by bringing in his own rhythm section: Dave Parlato on electric bass, Terry Bozzio on drums and Emil Richards on percussion.

At Royce Hall, 'Pedro's Dowry' was preceded by Zappa's narrative, a sequence of romantic cliches that ends in a 'cheap little fuck' where the lovers 'accidentally knock over an ashtray'. The music is appropriately 'cheesy', with all kinds of movie-score devices. 'Naval Aviation In Art' is a short string study; when it was re-recorded under the baton of Pierre Boulez for *The Perfect Stranger*, Zappa provided its storyline: an artist-sailor gazes through a porthole and paints a picture. 'Duke Of Prunes' is a setting of the tune from *Absolutely Free*. At Royce Hall, Tommy Morgan played a harmonica solo; Zappa replaced it with one of his guitar solos, using the studio-feedback set-up debuted on *Zoot Allures*.

Orchestral Favorites includes two tunes recorded at Royce Hall, but omitted from *Läther*: 'Strictly Genteel' and 'This Town Is A Sealed Tuna Sandwich'. The latter is renamed 'Bogus Pomp', a perfect description of the tongue-in-cheek, mocking way that 'classical' effects are arraigned and subverted. This is a lost gem in Zappa's oeuvre. His ear, practised in mixing in the studio, means that his score may deploy clichés, but he balances the sounds as if organising electronic music. His violins and clarinets sound like sine-waves, his piano like random chimes. The music is built out of a system of pauses and flurries. Zappa maintained that Edgard Varèse composed in the same way that Alexander Calder constructed his mobiles: by balancing sound blocks next to each other. You can hear Zappa do that on 'Bogus Pomp'. Tricks like contact-miking the violin and playing it through a wah-wah pedal transform standard orchestral sound. Some of it sounds as if Zappa took an eraser to the score, omitting expected sections and thereby achieving new orchestral relations. Prentis may be correct that much of *Orchestral Favorites* is more 'accessible' on *Läther*, but 'Bogus Pomp' is not to be missed: the 'Tuna' theme is forgotten as Zappa's glistening timbres revolve round each other like cogs in a magnificent, crazy machine. The thirteen-minutes of 'Bogus Pomp' finally twinkles off into xylophone chimes, leaving a magical silence in the air.

F R A N K Z A P P A
LÄTHER

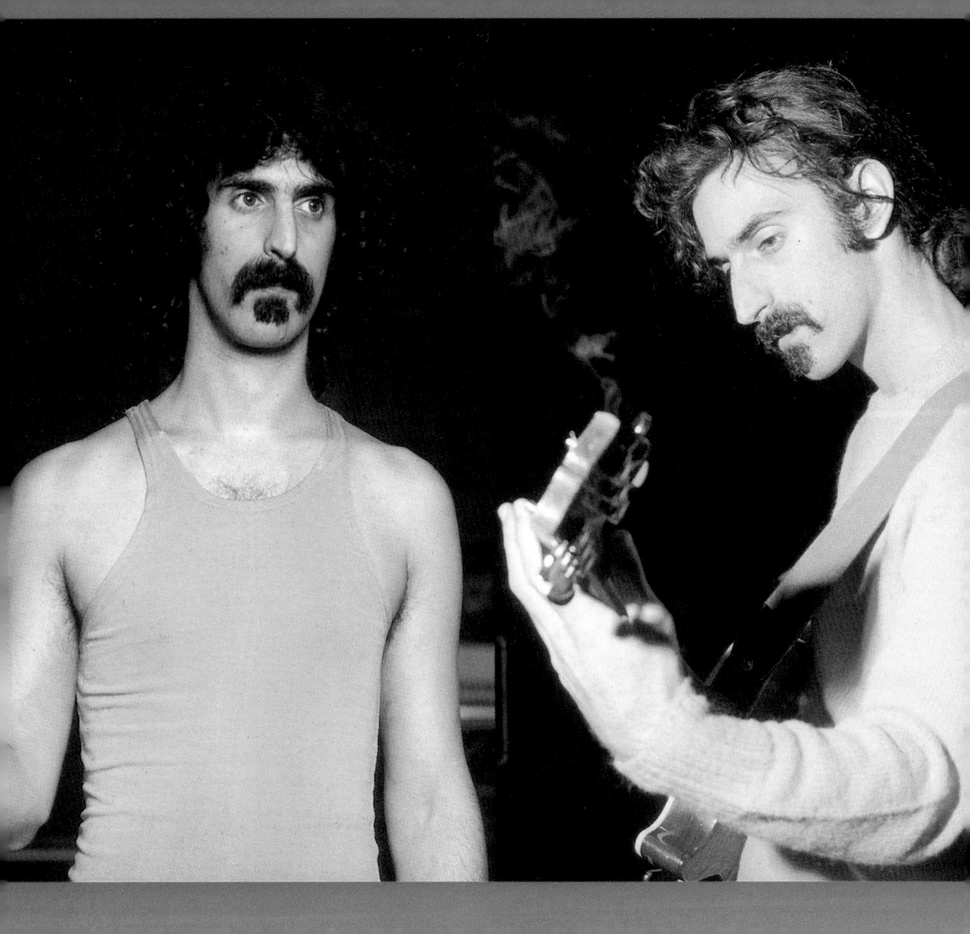

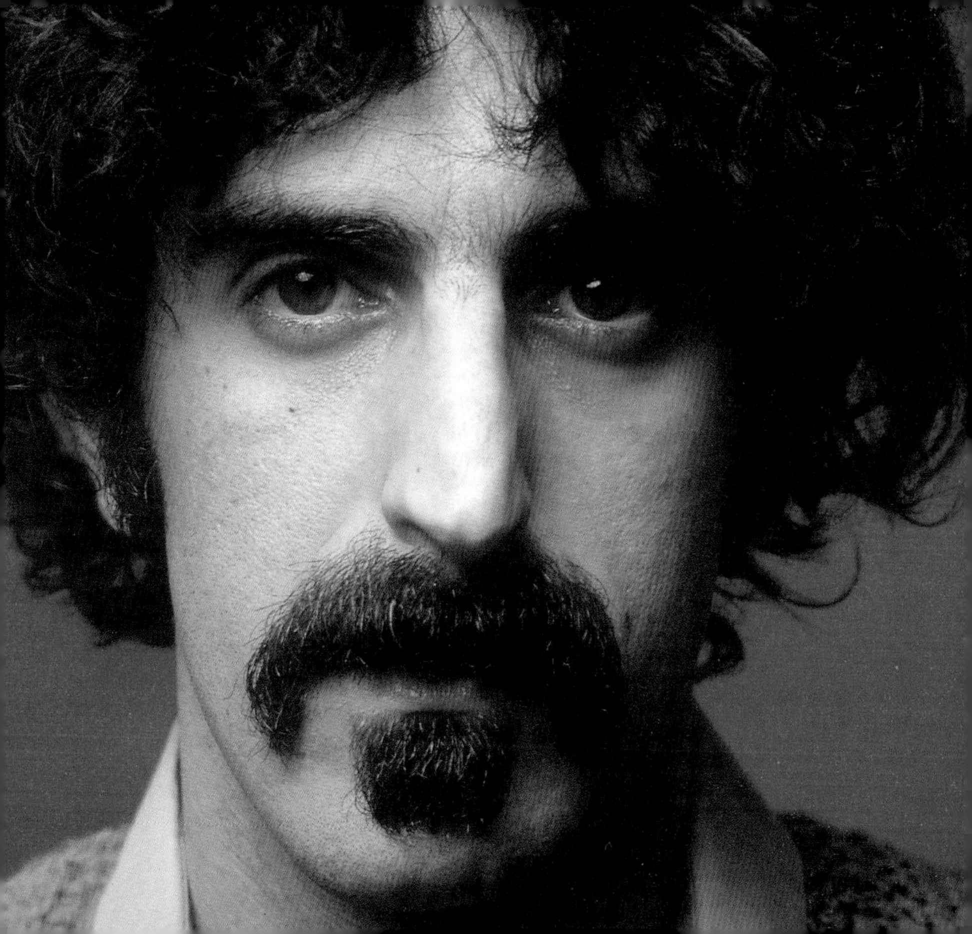

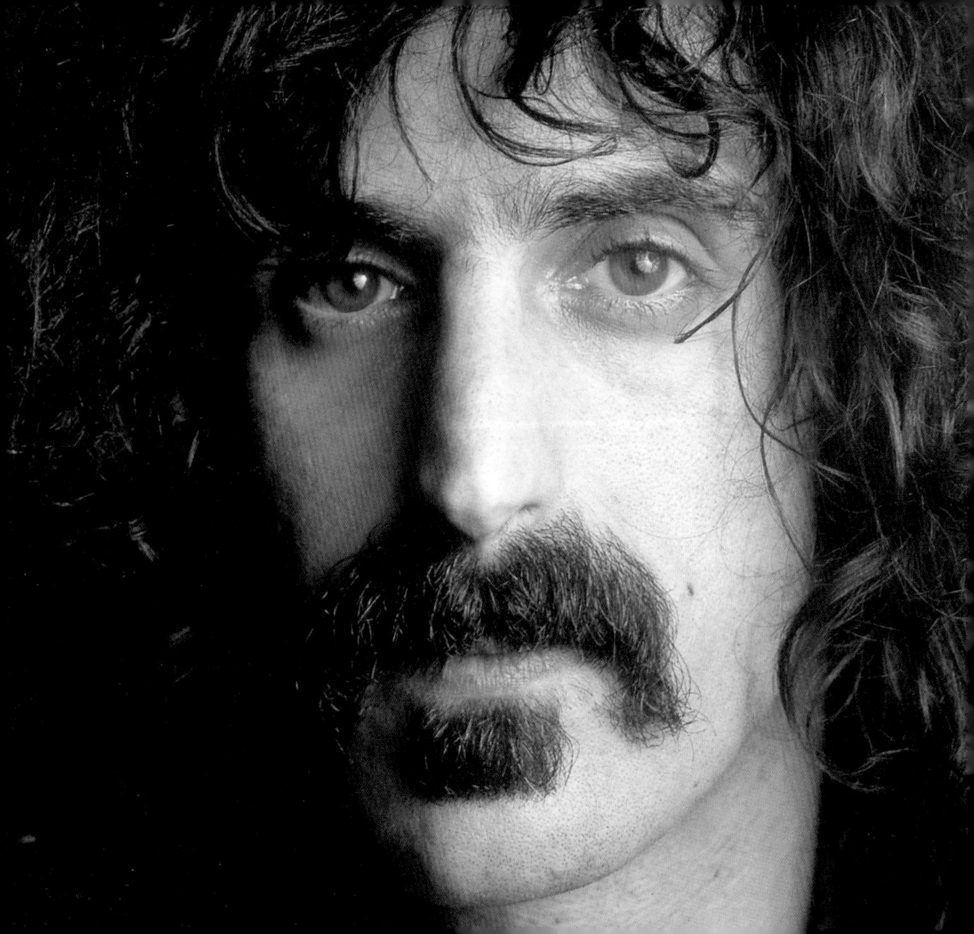

LÄTHER

(PLANNED RELEASE: NOVEMBER 1977;
FIRST RELEASE: SEPTEMBER 1996 RYKODISC/RCD 10574/76)

The original *Läther* project was four vinyl records in a box. After Zappa broadcast it on the radio for home-taping on 31 October 1977, it circulated among collectors as two C90 casettes. When Rykodisc released it posthumously in 1996, Frank's son Dweezil contributed a cover (a cow with markings that resemble the coastlines of Corsica, Italy and Sicily, home of Zappa Senior's ancestors), Gail Zappa wrote the story of *Läther's* 'curing', and Simon Prentis provided a track-by-track commentary. To make it a 3CD release, 'vaultmeister' Joe Travers went into the tape archive at Zappa's home studio and found some 'bonus tracks': some spoken-word from Zappa's 'bootleg this!' broadcast, a remix of 'Regyptian Strut' Zappa made in 1993, a guitar solo called 'Leather Goods' (a snippet of which occurs on *Läther* proper during 'Duck Duck Goose'), 'Revenge Of The Knick Knack People' (a 'ballet for piano, percussion and tape effects' recorded in 1978) and the non-vocal 'Time Is Money'. However, discographical complexities should not detract from the fact that, *Civilization Phaze III* notwithstanding, *Läther* was Zappa's VASTEST, MOST AMBITIOUS, MOST WIDE-RANGING AND MOST COMPLETE ARTWORK. Ever.

Läther's proper release was sabotaged from the very start, and already this 'Complete Guide' has muddied the waters by treating the content of *Läther* in its piecemeal occurence on actual releases, rather than in its envisaged unity. Introduced by a confessional adolescent stuttering 'I-I-leather!', *Läther* is an epic meditation on the meaning of rock music as a rite of passage in American society – and hence raises all the relevant questions about cultural maturity, and the place of sexual release and freedom in a society geared towards work.

In 1996, composer David Aldridge advanced the thesis that all of *Läther*'s music was based on Led Zeppelin's 'Whole Lotta Love' (itself a steal, of course, from Willie Dixon's 'You Need

Love'). On the 3CD release, the 'bonus track' 'Leather Goods' – the source of Zappa's citation of the 'Whole Lotta Love' riff on 'Duck Duck Down' – makes Aldridge's case still more persuasive: 'this track hammers away obsessively at the three-note cell and acts as a palimpsest for *Läther*. Even its most experimental tape collages find their source in the avant-garde noise-whirls at the centre of the Led Zeppelin track.' It is as if Zappa has held up a prism to the initial thrill generated by rock, and split it into all the sounds, impulses and possibilities it might harbour.

Aldridge gains independent confirmation from other Zappological arcana. According to Pamela Des Barres, the 'mudshark' story (see *Fillmore East June 1970* and *Apostrophe(')*) started with Led Zeppelin road-manager Richard Cole and John Bonham's exploits with a red snapper and a red-haired groupie. 'Fred Zeppelin' was a mooted title for a Zappa album (backstage passes for the 1980 US tour were printed with the slogan 'Fred Zeplinnn', but drummer John Bonham's death in September 1980 caused Zappa to shelve the idea). The version of 'Stairway To Heaven' on the 1988 tour – and its release as a 12" single with a cover photograph of staircases leading nowhere – showed that Led Zeppelin was an abiding obsession.

Apart from some of the intertrack collage, all the songs and tunes of *Läther* eventually gained legitimate release: 'A Little Green Rosetta' became the epic final track of *Joe's Garage*, while its closing guitar section (the coda to 'Black Napkins' performed at Osaka on 3 February 1976) became 'Ship Ahoy' on *Shut Up 'N' Play Yer Guitar*; 'Down In De Dew' appeared on a tape cassette issued by *Guitar World*; the title-track 'Läther' appeared on *Zappa In New York* as 'I Promise Not To Come In Your Mouth'.

Läther remains a compulsive knot in Zappa's oeuvre, such a fantastic, involuted conundrum that devotees end up purchasing all the other formats simply to have the pleasure of speculating about Zappa's intentions. But it remains a moot question whether the real way to experience *Läther* shouldn't be via the tape-swap 'loop' to which Zappa originally consigned it with his original radio broadcast: 'you can have it for free, just tape it off the air...'(Fair enough; after all Läther is the German for 'Ether' or 'air').

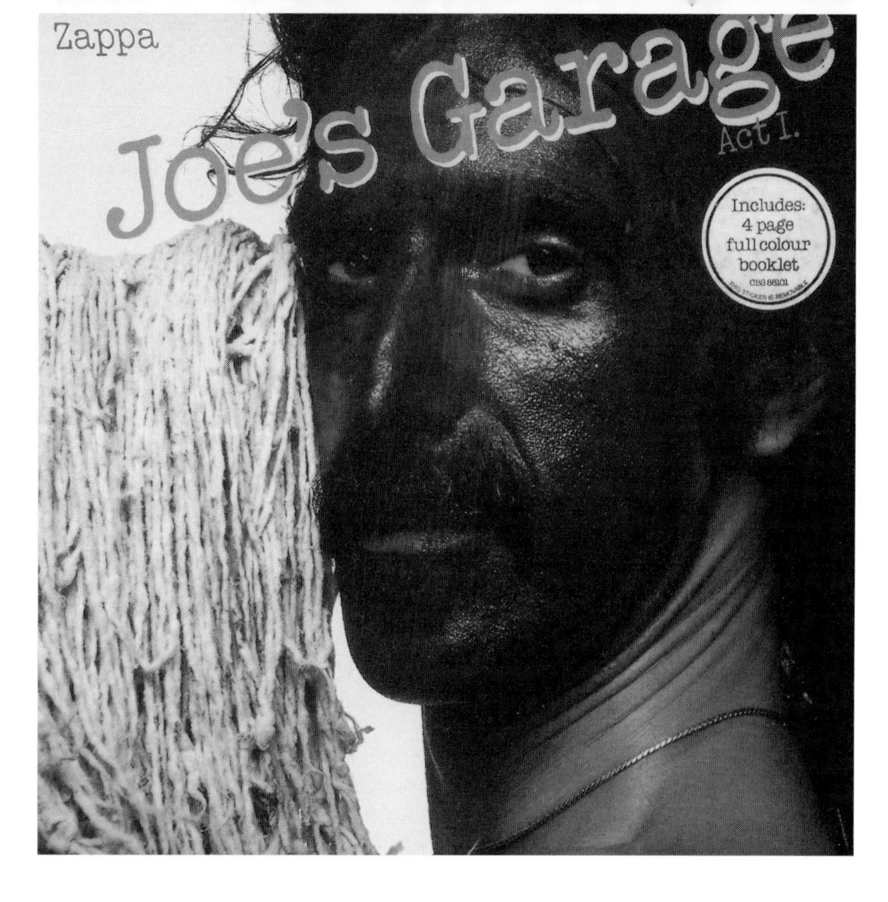
Zappa
Joe's Garage
Act I.
Includes:
4 page
full colour
booklet
CBS 86101
THIS STICKER IS REMOVABLE

JOE'S GARAGE ACTS I, II AND III

(ORIGINAL RELEASES: SEPTEMBER & NOVEMBER 1979;
CD RELEASE RYKODISC/RCD 10530/31)

Joe's Garage began its existence with Frank Zappa taking his band into the studio to cut a single: 'Joe's Garage', an account of rock's evolution from doo-wop to New Wave, backed by 'Catholic Girls', his obtuse riposte to the controversy surrounding 'Jewish Princess'. They ended up cutting sixteen tracks. Then, over a single weekend, he made up a story to provide continuity: 'it's like doing crossword puzzles', he said. Figuring that the cost of a triple album 'might be hard on people the way the world is today', *Joe's Garage* was released as a single album (Act I) in September 1979 (with gatefold sleeve, extensive dadaist visuals and fold-out lyric sheet), followed by a double album (Acts II & III) two months later. Sleevenotes, stage directions and graphics encouraged listeners to lose themselves in the detail of it all. Zappa-heads who started in the early 80s invariably cite it as a favourite.

'It's sort of like a really cheap kind of high school play... the way it might have been done 20 years ago, with all the sets made out of cardboard boxes and poster paints.' Zappa never lost his affection for representation that gives way at the seams, and *Joe's Garage* is full of it. His own between-track commentary – the voice of the 'Central Scrutinizer' – makes fluffs and blunders, creating a comedy-record dishevellment that distracts from some extremely well-made music. As he said on the closing track, after he decides to turn off the plastic megaphone that created the voice of the Central Scrutinizer and speak in his regular voice: 'they're pretty good musicians, but it don't make no difference if they're good musicians, because anybody who would buy this record doesn't give a fuck if there's good musicians on it, because this is a stupid song – AND THAT'S THE WAY I LIKE IT'.

Joe's Garage debuted singer Ike Willis, whose light, insinuating voice marks Zappa's late music as indelibly as Ray Collins marked the music of the Mothers Of Invention. Willis was studying at Washington University in St Louis when Zappa played there on 2 October 1977, and inveigled himself onto the stage crew. Zappa found out he was a singer, and tried him out on 'Bamboozled By Love' and 'Carolina Hardcore Ecstasy', then asked him for his phone number so he could attend the next auditions. As his own album *Shoulda Gone Before I Left* shows, Willis is a political animal (in 1988, onstage remarks about 'confinement loaf' – a proposal to give drugged bread to state prisoners – stemmed from an article Willis read in *Washington Post*), as well as being fond of word play (the word 'plook' is credited to him on *Joe's Garage*). An ideal Zappa collaborator.

The songs were the kind of Zappa 'filth' that drove contemporary *NME* journalists into frenzies of righteous indignation. The storyline followed Dale Bozzio's Mary and her evolution from Catholic Girl to Crew Slut and then Wet T-Shirt contestant (perhaps the journalists missed that her 'mammalian protuberances' were being viewed 'through a thoroughly soaked, stupid-looking white sort of male person's conservative kind of middle-of-the-road' ideology). Apart from 'Watermelon In Easter Hay', all the guitar solos on the album were applied 'xenochronously' to alien backing tracks. 'Wet T-Shirt Nite' (renamed 'Fembot In A Wet T-Shirt' on the CD) itself contained some stunning examples of Zappa's tortuous metrics. Act I ends with Ike Willis's interpretation of the title track from Jeff Simmons' *Lucille Has Messed My Mind Up*, drawing it into Luther Vandross territory.

'A Token Of My Extreme' was a tune played by the *Roxy & Elsewhere* band (it gave a name to a brilliant TV special). Here the lyrics satirised L. Ron Hubbard and Scientology, leading to the kaballistic obscenity of 'Stick It Out' and its reprise of both *Sheik Yerbouti*'s dumb chat-up lines (described in the booklet as 'traditional American Love Poetry') and *Fillmore East June 1970*'s 'Latex Solar

Beef'. 'Sy Borg' was a tale of technological fetishism that, like the autonomous sex-acts of *Zoot Allures*, reflects on Zappa's own mode of musical production: without the latest sound equipment, *Joe's Garage* would have been impossible to realise. The tingles and swoops of Peter Wolf's synth solo constitute an evocation of oral sex to set besides Jobson's solo on 'I Promise Not To Come In Your Mouth' (*Zappa In New York*).

'Dong Work For Uda' was a song for Zappa's bodyguard John Smothers, whose mispronunciations were legendary. Such wordplay climaxed in the 'negrocious' dialect of *Thing-Fish*. 'Keep It Greasey', a song about the delights of heterosexual anality, was reconfigured to describe Joe's treatment in a special prison where they keep 'the other criminals from the music business... you know... the ones who get caught'. Like Dante in the *Inferno*, the artist was meting out imaginary revenge on all his enemies. The aptly titled 'Outside Now' featured further guitar xenochrony. 'Packard Goose' was Zappa's tirade against punk-enthused music-journalists, with plentiful xenochronous guitar 'imagined' by Joe, who has now left prison only to discover a dystopia of welfare bureaucracy and mounds of 'dead consumer goods'.

'Watermelon In Easter Hay' was one of three guitar pieces – along with 'Black Napkins' and 'Zoot Allures' – to which the Zappa Family Trust retained the rights as constituting the 'soul' of Frank Zappa (in January 1997, Dweezil Zappa re-released them on CD, with three unreleased live versions and 'Merely A Blues In A', on the mail-order UMRK label). It's very pretty music, Zappa accepting harmonic conventions he normally derided. After this lapse into 'untrammelled lyricism', Zappa's dadaist instincts won out, and he finished with the shambolic 'humour' of 'A Little Green Rosetta'. Some Zappologists interpret the latter as a comment on 'beauty': a useless, kitsch ornament 'pooted forth' on the meaningless repetitions of our workaday lives.

FRANK ZAPPA
TINSELTOWN REBELLION

TINSEL TOWN REBELLION

(ORIGINAL RELEASE: MAY 1981;
CD RELEASE RYKODISC/RCD 10532)

Cal Schenkel's cover portrayed Zappa as bemused entertainer with civilisation toppling around his ears. Decadent army officers in dress uniform swig champagne from the bottle. It's like a scene by Georg Grosz, showing how military escalation benefits certain social sectors. Considering that the Reagan/Thatcher era of high unemployment, massive arms spending and yuppie arrogance was just starting, some found Zappa's words in 'The Blue Light' – 'Death Valley Days, straight ahead' – disturbingly prescient. Zappa's anti-war single, 'I Don't Want To Get Drafted', was refused distribution by CBS.

'Fine Girl' is iconic sexism, linking such attitudes to reggae and pre-industrial motifs like thong sandals and carrying water from the well. 'Easy Meat' is more iconic sexism, including a section of 'massive overdubbage' where Tommy Mars shows that Heavy Metal and Classical use identical flourishes to build to climaxes. Zappa's skill at montage was undiminished. A harpsichord chord and a whispered 'they're just not going to stand for it' introduced 'Titties & Beer' on *Läther*. Here it introduces a monumental solo where Zappa's guitar appears to be improvising the music's very structure. Vinnie Colaiuta was such a mobile and responsive drummer he enabled Zappa to move the whole ensemble with each whammy-bar assertion.

'For The Young Sophisticate' was a new version of the *Läther* tune, this time heavy with silly-sounding marimbas as Zappa satirised peer-group pressure. 'Love Of My Life' from *Ruben & The Jets* and 'I Ain't Got No Heart' from *Freak Out!* were chances for Zappa to demonstrate the power and velocity of his latest band. 'Panty Rap' saw Zappa collecting articles of female underwear for artist Emily James to sew into a quilt. Zappologist Jonathan Jones took this to be quite literally 'showing America's dirty linen in public', and a perfect illustration of Zappa's 'collage' aesthetic. It also introduced the panty-sniffing theme, as the ever-horny musicians passed round the undergarments. 'Tell Me You Love Me' is the hysterical expression of lust from *Chunga's Revenge* that became satire on Michael Jackson in *Broadway The Hard Way*.

'Now You See It – Now You Don't' is a guitar solo, once again illustrating Colaiuta's invention and mobility. 'Dance Contest', like 'Panty Rap', was a slice of onstage antics. Rykodisc's lyric-sheet introduces a confusing error; Zappa actually says 'If you're out there and you're cute, maybe you're beautiful, I just want to tell you somethin' – there's more of us ugly mother-fuckers than you are...'. Although correctly transcribed in the vinyl gatefold, this now reads 'and you're not cute...', which makes a nonsense of Zappa's consistent anti-glamour position.

'The Blue Light' pilloried post-hippie inertia with an extraordinary combination of free-association and effects. Zappa defends the authentic Italian pizza and prophesizes Reaganite doom. 'Tinsel Town Rebellion' attacked punk, citing the 'Sunshine Of Your Love' riff at the mention of 'cream'. 'Bamboozled By Love' is a vivid dissection of psychotic jealousy. 'Brown Shoes Don't Make It' from *Absolutely Free* was another boast about the skill and discipline of Zappa's band; 'Peaches III' (so-called because Zappa had twice recorded it before: on *Hot Rats* and on *Fillmore East*) sounded thin and extra perverse in Zappa's new version.

Zappa had never issued a record so full of old tunes before. His '80s schedule of endless touring – an approach that allowed him to stay in the public eye and realise his orchestral projects despite zero radio exposure and no 'hits' – demanded that his musicians became conversant with his entire catalogue. At the close of the album, following up his patriotic remarks about pizza, Zappa had guitarist Warren Cucurullo pay tribute to a list of 'great Italians'. The names included Conlon Nancarrow, who wasn't Italian at all, but whose avantgarde compositions for player pianos were providing Zappa with inspiration to pursue xenochrony into uncharted waters. *Tinsel Town Rebellion* was the boast of a band-leader who refused to let commercial viability become a brake on musical innovation.

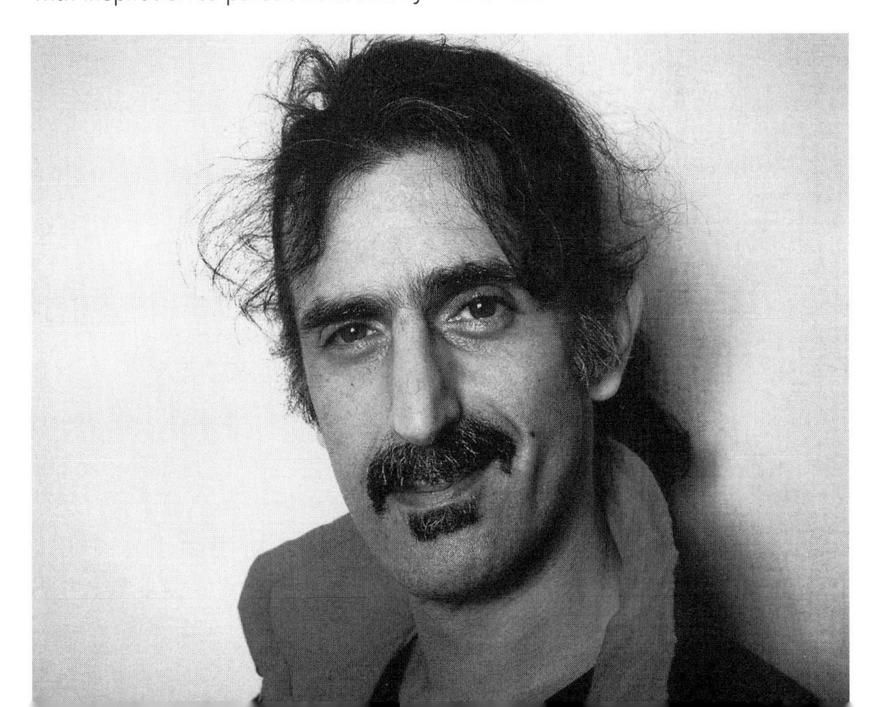

Shut Up 'n Play Yer Guitar

SHUT UP 'N' PLAY YER GUITAR

(ORIGINAL RELEASE: MAY 1981;
CD RELEASE RYKODISC/RCD 10533/34/35)

Zappa's emergence as a guitar hero was a known only to those who attended his concerts. Music papers which had seen falling circulations revivified by Punk – New Musical Express and Sounds – damned guitar solos as 'hippie self-indulgence' (writers who disagreed that the punk revolution meant denouncing any music that didn't fit pop formats, notably Richard Cook and Graham Lock, split to join The Wire, which became house journal of the 80s 'jazz revival'). Meanwhile, the American mainstream rock press lauded an absurd series of Heavy Metal guitar heroes in spandex and stack-heels. Shut Up 'N' Play Yer Guitar was designed to teach the journos a lesson. The original box-set included these fighting words on the back:

'Until the release of this album, only a few people realised what the hardcore fanatics had known all along... that FZ can play the guitar. While the papers and magazines shouted the praises of every other fashionable guitar strangler and condemned Zappa for having the guts to sing lyrics they thought were disgusting, he quietly continued to say things on his instrument that were far more blasphemous than any words could convey. In the rush to be offended by what he said, the music press forgot to listen to what his guitar was talking about. Zappa's guitar solos, as captured in this album, say a lot of things that just might prove to be embarrassing to the writers who forgot to listen.'

The Rykodisc edition – otherwise a miniature replica of the vinyl box-set, leading to short playing times on each CD – replaced this text by John Swenson's review from *Guitar World* (November 1981). Swenson made apposite remarks about the relationship of Zappa's guitar playing to conceptual continuity, and gave a detailed exposition of xenochrony. However, this technique was not used on *Shut Up*; these are all documents of solos with realtime accompaniment, albeit sliced from context. Zappologists have fun working out which tunes they come from: the three 'Shut Up' title-tracks and 'Gee, I Like Your Pants' come from 'Inca Roads'; 'five-five-FIVE' from 'Conehead'; 'Hog Heaven' and 'Soup And Old Clothes' from 'The Illinois Enema Bandit'; 'Variations On The Carlos Santana Secret Chord Progression' from 'If Only She Woulda'; 'Ship Ahoy' (the conclusion to 'A Little Green Rosetta' on *Läther*) and 'Pink Napkins' from 'Black Napkins'; 'Pinnochio's Furniture' from 'Chunga's Revenge'.

To provide relief, Zappa broke up the tracks with snippets of spoken-word and 'mouth-noises' from *Läther*, plus some intimate studio work: 'While You Were Out', 'Stucco Homes' and 'Canard Du Jour'. The latter is a charming 'ethnological forgery' recorded by Kerry McNabb at Paramount Studios in the mid-70s, with Jean-Luc Ponty on breathy baritone violin and Zappa playing bouzouki.

Strangely enough, Zappa reported that *Shut Up 'N' Play Yer Guitar*, originally only a mail-order item, actually sold better than *Tinsel Town Rebellion* and the subsequent *You Are What You Is*. Situated in a strange place in the culture – after punk, rock was meant to be a place for songs and statements rather than musicianship – *Shut Up 'N' Play Yer Guitar* elevated Zappa's guitar status to the select pantheon of 80s originals that includes Blood Ulmer, Bill Frisell and Skip McDonald.

YOU
ARE
WHAT
YOU
IS

YOU ARE WHAT YOU IS

(ORIGINAL RELEASE: SEPTEMBER 1981;
CD RELEASE RYKODISC/RCD 10536)

The publicity Barking Pumpkin produced for You Are What You Is brimmed with confidence: 'Containing 20 of the most exciting studio recordings since whenever... on an album stylistically in the region of We're Only In It For The Money by way of Sheik Yerbouti and that means this is going to be THE BIG ONE...'. Still more than Tinsel Town Rebellion, this record was aimed at the rock audience, with punchy songs, complete lyric-sheet and conceptual continuities designed to fascinate the teen consumer. Like Tinsel Town, it was ignored by radio DJs due to its scurrility and politics.

Ever aware of the limits of dissent in a society dedicated to the pursuit of profit, Zappa took the opportunity to air an article he'd written for *Newsweek* magazine, but which had been rejected as too 'idiosyncratic'. In the double-vinyl release, it was printed in colour inside the gatefold sleeve, the word 'cheese' picked out in yellow, and Zappa's coinage for the bottom line of profit – 'the prime rate poodle' – picked out in red (in 1981, before Desk Top Publishing allowed magazines to make wilful decisions about font and colour, this looked pretty outlandish). 'Yes, Virginia... there is a FREE LUNCH' summarised the complacency of a management class living off the labour of others.

Consistent to his antagonistic ethic, Zappa began with a song that directly abused his intended audience, *Freak Out!*'s 'You're Probably Wondering Why I'm Here' re-equipped for the 80s: 'Teen-age Wind' had an endless chorus 'we want to be free, as free as the wind'. The song's repetitions were designed to show how unfree adolescent aspirations actually were. Jimmy Carl Black guested, reciting key lines from *200 Motels* and singing country'n'western on 'Harder Than Your Husband'. 'Doreen' was doo-wop pleadery pumped up into arena pomp. 'Goblin Girl' celebrated girls who can 'gobble it all' to a tune that was an extension of 'Jewish Princess' and 'Catholic Girls'. Asides about skin colour and fish skin predicted *Thing-Fish*. 'Theme From The 3rd Movement Of Sinister Footwear' seemed like a bizarre title for a guitar solo – until you learn it was a theme from one of Zappa's 'ballet's (as conducted by Kent Nagano at the Zellerbach Auditorium on 16 June 1984).

Although Zappa called *You Are What You Is* a 'studio recording', he followed his habit of overdubbing tracks that were recorded live. The sequence 'Society Pages' through to 'Conehead' (side two of the original vinyl) was frequently played as a suite. 'You Are What You Is' – a title that uses bad grammar to raise questions about social identity – mocked racial insecurities; 'Mudd Clubb', like *Tinsel Town*'s 'The Blue Light', drew political conclusions from the absurdities contemporary America required for sexual gratification (in his sleevenote to *Läther*, Simon Prentis explains the 'lather' word by reference to the 'sudsy yellow nozzle of their foaming nocturnal... ejactamenta' in 'Mudd Club').

'The Meek Shall Inherit Nothing' and 'Heavenly Bank Account' were assaults on religion, while 'Dumb All Over' voiced fears about Christian Fundamentalism and American hysteria about Islam. 'Drafted Again' – a remake of the suppressed 'I Don't Want To Get Drafted' single – saw where all this might lead. Zappa's 1980 world-tour programme recycled Schenkel's anti-war graphic from the back of the single. The American eagle and the Russian bear confront each other over an atomic explosion. Over the top it asked: 'Is this trip really necessary?' (this wartime slogan was printed over an image of a family in a car, home propaganda designed to reduce domestic consumption of petrol). The song ends with a sped-up, munchkin voice howling 'leave my nose alone, please'. Zappologist Jonathan Jones points out that this recalls Zappa's childhood treatments for sinus trouble, which involved 'stuffing radium into your sinus cavities' on the end of 'a foot-length piece of wire'. As with the dentist chair pictured in the Uncle Meat gatefold, Zappa was attempting to shock his audience into acknowledgment of the realities of war by reminding them of their own personal experiences of pain, however trivial.

Ship arriving too late to save a drowning witch

SHIP ARRIVING TOO LATE TO SAVE A DROWNING WITCH

(ORIGINAL RELEASE: MAY 1982; CD RELEASE RYKODISC/RCD 10537)

To see the first and last letters of Zappa's name in the initial letters of Zoot Allures might seem far-fetched, but Drowning Witch showed that Zappa had a kaballist's fascination for the position of his name in the alphabet. The cover showed one of Roger Price's 'droodies' (a book of which was published in Los Angeles in 1953): by writing his name above using triangles for 'a', Zappa showed how he'd seen the first and last letters of his name -- 'ZA' – in Price's puzzle picture of a 'ship arriving too late to save a drowning witch' (or, alternatively 'a mother pyramid feeding its child').

On *200 Motels*, Rance Muhammitz asked the Lord to have mercy on the 'mind of the man in the street'; the graphics of *Joe's Garage* showed the daydreams of toilet cleaners, housewives, lab-technicians and bell-boys; the opener to *Drowning Witch*, 'No Not Now', portrays the sexual quandaries of a truck driver. 'Valley Girl' – a surprise novelty hit – featured Zappa's daughter Moon mimicking the inanities of San Fernando Valley little rich girls. 'I Come From Nowhere' had Roy Estrada, bassist for the original Mothers, Beefheart and Little Feat, singing in a gruesome falsetto, as Zappa depicted the grimaces of fraudulent, ever-smiling TV-oriented personalities and politicians.

The title track extended Price's memorable phrase into a staggering twelve-minute composition. It began with what Zappa was calling 'melt-down' – lyrics recited to indeterminate pitch. Zappa scatted the theme from Stravinsky's *The Rite Of Spring* (appropriately enough, a ballet about ritual sacrifice), and then launched into his own proof that the 'present-day composer refuses to die'. Zappa's infolding of arena-rock guitar and intricately-detailed avantgarde percusion is unique in the divided history of twentieth-century music. 'Envelopes' was yet more perverse composition, while 'Teenage Prostitute', sung by opera singer Lisa Popiel (also responsible for 'Lisa's Life Story' on *You Can't Do That On Stage Anymore Vol.6*), is a blast of frenzied rock'n'roll, shrieking with hysteria: the other side of Hollywood life from Valley-girl vacancy.

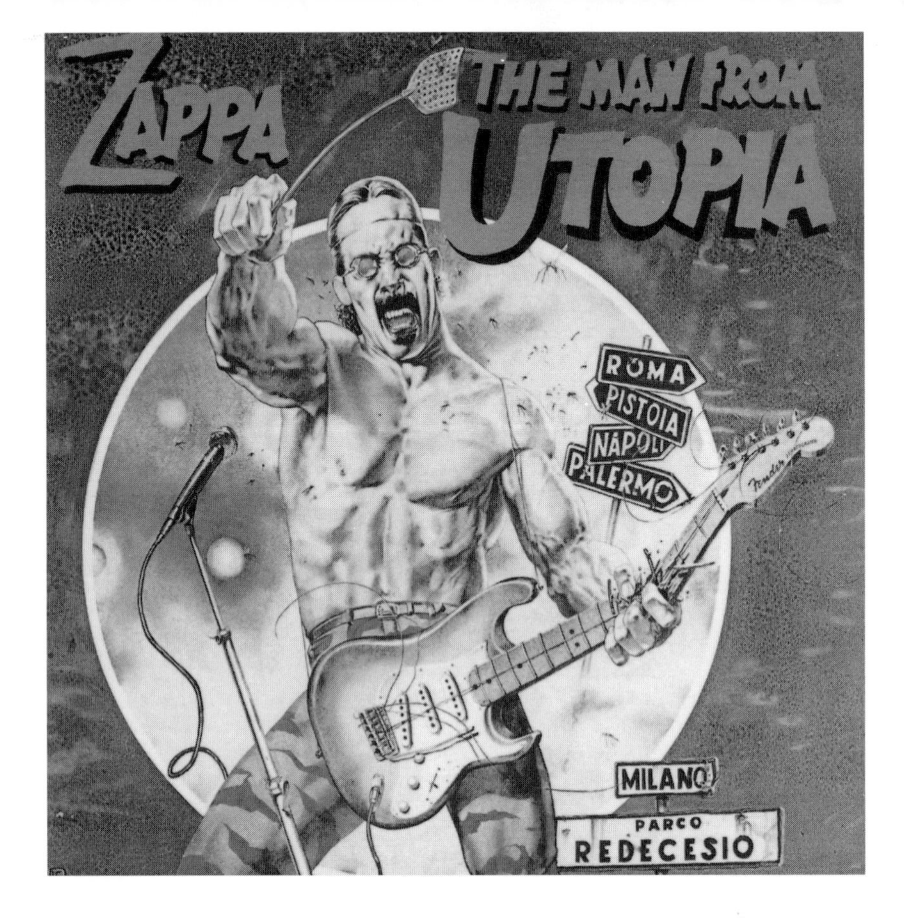
ZAPPA
THE MAN FROM
UTOPIA
ROMA
PISTOIA
NAPOLI
PALERMO
MILANO
PARCO
REDECESIO

THE MAN FROM UTOPIA

(ORIGINAL RELEASE: MARCH 1983;
CD RELEASE RYKODISC/RCD 10538)

On Man From Utopia, by general consent, Zappa's ability to foment the annoyance factor reached a climax. However, as with all Zappa's grotesques, it finds its supporters. Engineer Spencer Chrislu's digital remix from 1992 considerably improved a somewhat understated, dry sound and made it lusher and larger. 'Cocaine Decisions' was given an extra minute, allowing the backing track's felicities to emerge from behind Zappa's lead vocal. An unreleased track, 'Luigi & The Wise Guys', allowed Roy Estrada's 'pachuco falsetto' to indulge garage doo-wop stylings in a manner that hadn't been heard since the original Mothers Of Invention ('double dork butt rash' replacing the 'bup bup showah doowah' of Andrew Lloyd Webber's concept of the period).

Zappa's patented 'meltdown' vocalising became ubiquitous: 'I'd start talking in a singsong tone of voice, and then Tommy Mars would chop changes behind it.' 'Dangerous Kitchen' had pre-written lyrics, but was performed with 'variable pitches and variable rhythms'. Its account of the 'stinky and squirty' sponge and 'frightful' salad has a leering, ludicrous quality only Zappa could achieve. 'The Jazz Discharge Party Hats', Zappa's improvised account of band members' panty-sniffing exploits, caused the usually imperturbable Neil Slaven to pronounce 'probably the most tasteless song in Frank's whole catalogue'. The fact that every note of his wobbling vocal line is being doubled by Steve Vai on guitar adds a ridiculous touch, like someone outlining a sheet stain in gold leaf. 'The Radio Is Broken' returned to the topic of budget sci-fi movies (see 'Cheepnis' on *Roxy & Elsewhere* and 'Debra Kadabra' on *Bongo Fury*), a weave of silly voices unheard since 'Be In My Video' on *Them Or Us*.

'SEX' is offensive glamour-critique, as Zappa explains that the emphasis on a fat-free existence is stupid because 'the bigger the cushion, the better the pushin'... who wants to ride on an ironin' board?'. 'Tink Walks Amok' was an instrumental feature for bassist Art Barrow, with the involuted melody lines and perverse metrics that are Zappa's trademark. 'We Are Not Alone', powered by Marty Krystall's baritone saxophone, is a gem, alternating as it does between the forward motion of the sax and fidgetting, fill-in sections of marimba and guitar. 'Moggio', named for baby Diva's dream about a tiny father who lived beneath her pillow, again demonstrated Zappa's compositional mastery of tension and release. If you can hear through the 'humour' of *Man From Utopia* to its material ingredients, one begins to grasp how truly strange it is. Zappa's confrontation of accident and rigour bears comparison to John Cage and Jackson Pollock and their fascination with 'chance'. However, although the Neo-dadaists of Fluxus liked to say they were demolishing 'high art' values, the discourse that surrounded them elevated them to a plane Zappa could not aspire to. Hence the relevance, at the very moment that he was perpetrating outrages like 'The Jazz Discharge Party Hats', of the 'classical' music Zappa was composing (see next chapter).

'CLASSICAL' PROJECTS

The thesis of this Complete Guide is that Zappa's work needs to be understood as a whole. His art was so manifold and subversive of genre that attempts to isolate the 'good' records from the 'bad' invariably tell us more about the limits of the critic than they do about Zappa's failings as an artist. However, for reasons of tidiness (and to give the narrative some shape), this chapter looks at the 'classical' projects that Zappa achieved between 1983 and 1993.

Nevertheless, it must be borne in mind that during this period, Zappa's 'rock' releases and world tours were relentless. One memorable rock title – *Them Or Us* – expressed the divide Zappa saw between the Christian Fundamentalists, eager to censor rock, soul and rap records – and the opposing constituency. He wanted to show that someone who wasn't a snob could write orchestral music, but he never doubted where he stood – with those dismissed as oiks, freaks and failures by the powers that be. Zappa's experience of social rejection at high school ran deep. As he sang on 'Cocaine Decisions', 'you are a person who is high class, you are a person not in my class'. Unlike many seduced by upwardly-mobile artforms, Zappa never discarded his delinquent principles.

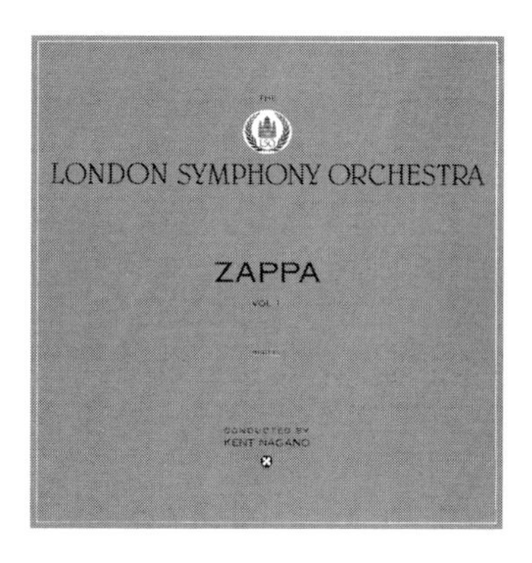

LONDON SYMPHONY ORCHESTRA VOL. 1 & 2

(ORIGINAL RELEASES: JUNE 1983 & SEPTEMBER & 1987;

CD RELEASE RYKODISC/RCD 10540/41)

London Symphony Orchestra Vol. 1 arrived in a grey cover, Zappa's name and that of the orchestra embossed on the cardboard. Inside, a shiny black inner sleeve imparted important information in white lettering: conductor Kent Nagano's academic resumé and a listing of the vintage of each string instrument played. All this assured the purchaser that this was a proper classical record. So 'proper', in fact, that it looked phony (a typical Zappa touch). The problem was that, by the 1980s, classical music was no longer a 'proper' tradition anyway.

In the postwar years, Boulez and Stockhausen had tried to reinvent the European tradition, but their innovations were rejected by the 'serious music' audience as being noisy and unlistenable (in *The Real Frank Zappa Book*, Zappa recounts wanting to shout 'sit down assholes, this is one of the real guys' as half the Lincoln Center walked out of a Boulez concert). The Minimalism of Steve Reich and Philip Glass – characterised by Zappa as 'mononchromonotony' – removed all the 'difficulty' of modern music, and offered nothing much instead (apart from confirmation of the cultural status of the concert-goer). From the start, Zappa insisted that there was something fantastic about Varèse and Stravinsky that had nothing to do with snob values. Zappa's vision was never going to fit the '80s, when postmodern relativism and commercial cynicism were the bright 'new' ideas. His 'classical' music was conceived as an assault on the heartland of snobbery.

London Symphony Orchestra Vol. 1 and its successor, released five years later, are weird experiences. The listener is immersed in an orchestral soup devoid of the fierce angularity of Zappa's other music. Anyone hoping for the violence and abstraction of Edgard Varèse will be disappointed. On the Rykodisc double-issue, 'Bob In Dacron' – originally relegated to Vol.2 – is programmed first. It's an off-putting opener, as it lacks either coherence or sparkle. However, the orchestral world according to Frank Zappa repays perseverence. 'Sad Jane' is chilling, as woodwinds state the eerie theme over plucked strings. Even in the midst of the most arrogant guitar bluster, Zappa always retained a certain claustrophobic poignancy, and here that emotion is distilled in its purest form.

In *The Real Frank Zappa Book*, Zappa mocks academic rules in whatever guise – serial or minimalist – and declares allegiance to timbre (sheer sound) as the carrier of musical meaning. That is how he organises his orchestral music – balancing little clarinet twiddles against brass snores, percussion passages that give way to swamping strings. Unlike Varèse, he doesn't avoid melody, harmony or sections of expressive 'tune-making', but these are never 'developed' either classically or serially. Sounds go out into the air to be contrasted and weighed next to other sounds, an aural equivalent to Kurt Schwitters and his Merzbau – an abstract art constructed out of litter and debris. It is as if Zappa is pondering the significance of the aural 'icons' he has collated.

At least, that's true of disc one ('Bob In Dacron', 'Sad Jane' and 'Mo 'n Herb's Vacation'). Disc two is less fragmentary and meditative. 'Envelopes' needs to be contrasted to the 'rock' version on *Drowning Witch*; 'Pedro's Dowry' welds chintzy motifs into its narrative of sexual seduction. 'Bogus Pomp' concatenates tunes from *200 Motels*. For anyone familiar with that music, it provides a delirious example of Zappa's ability to make instrumental timbre recall verbal phrases. 'Strictly Genteel' is a perfect summation of the absurdities of high culture in an industrial age.

As composer David Aldridge has pointed out, Zappa's technique is heavily dependent on movie clichés, and he rarely achieves the magical transformations of 'spectral' composers like Gerard Grisey, Tristan Murail or James Dillon. Zappa admits as much in a sleevenote. However, Aldridge rightly praises Zappa's surging melodies and hilarious contrasts of noise and harmony as aspects missing from most European 'serious' composition (or indeed the 'populist' American composers who have arrived in the wake of Minimalism). Pierre Boulez was pointing to the same thing when he remarked on the 'vitality' of Zappa's scores.

American Artist: Donald Roller Wilson

BOULEZ
CONDUCTS
ZAPPA

The Perfect
Stranger

and other chamber works
performed by the
ENSEMBLE
INTERCONTEMPORAIN
and the
BARKING PUMPKIN
DIGITAL
GRATIFICATION
CONSORT

THE PERFECT STRANGER

(ORIGINAL RELEASE: AUGUST 1984;
CD RELEASE RYKODISC/RCD 10542)

Billed as 'Boulez Conducts Zappa', The Perfect Stranger was not only the fulfilment of one of Zappa's ambitions – avantgarde composer Pierre Boulez was listed among the many 'influences' on Freak Out! – it is also a strong musical statement. Unlike the London Symphony Orchestra, Pierre Boulez's Ensemble InterContemporain was a smallish ensemble dedicated to playing innovative music. In The Real Frank Zappa Biook, Zappa takes a cynical look at the modern classical scene: its one-off 'premières' that are under-rehearsed, its false smiles and PR hypocrisy. He implies that the performances of 'The Perfect Stranger', 'Naval Aviation In Art?' and 'Dupreee's Paradise' were inadequate. On the record, though, Zappa thanks Boulez for 'having the patience to demand accurate performance of the killer triplets on page eight'. The real test has to be how this music sounds, and to these ears, it sounds good. The Perfect Stranger does not have the hesitations or muzziness that characterise unengaged playing.

Zappa wrote humoresque stories to accompany his pieces (declaring, perhaps defensively in the presence of the great M. Boulez, that they were 'preposterously non-modern' and 'for entertainment purposes only'). 'The Perfect Stranger' has a vacuum-cleaner salesman sprinkle 'demonstration dirt' on the carpet for a slovenly housewife, all watched by Patricia, 'the dog in the high chair' (this referred to the cover painting by Donald Roller Wilson, whose sick/surreal aesthetic inspired 'Evelyn, A Modified Dog' on *One Size Fits All*). Zappa's cartoon-like narrative rubbishes high-art seriousness, yet proved a challenge for Boulez's musicians (Boulez later said that the very difficulty of these scores was good for his musicians).

'Naval Aviation In Art?' is a short piece all about tension and sustain. The Ensemble's string players interpret it beautifully. 'Dupree's Paradise' is a composition from the *Roxy* era which the band performed as a jazz burlesque (see *You Can't Do That On Stage Anymore Vol.2*). The Ensemble turn it into a haunting, shiny mechanism full of lingering sighs and sad transitions.

The rest of the pieces on *The Perfect Stranger* show what a present-day composer could do with a Synclavier (a digital music-editing suite). Zappa lifts off from what's he's learned by working with musicians: 'The Girl In The Magnesium Dress' is constructed from xylophone and marimba samples that recall Art Tripp and Ruth Underwood, trickles and runs weaving in and out of impossible ambiences. 'Love Story' purported to show an 'elderly Republican couple attempting sex while break-dancing' – fifty-five seconds of boings and bed-springs. 'Outside Now Again' is a setting of the pentatonic melody from *Joe's Garage*, showing the pastoral lyricism that links Zappa to Canterbury Rock. Something splendid and oriental lurks in the tune too. 'Jonestown', named for the site of a mass-suicide by religious fanatics, is not shorter in the CD than the vinyl release as widely believed (the record lists it as 7:07 rather than 5:27 erroneously). It is one of Zappa's most chilling statements. Its anti-religious message is voiced in sinister, '50s-movie 'spooky' strings and gloomy religious chants. Against this drab, grey-green wash there are clattering, metallic 'events' that resemble serial processes in Messiaen and Boulez: their brave, enlightened music lives on in Zappa's Synclavier.

DONALD ROLLER WILSON·1983/24
AUGUST 22·MONDAY·6:48 P.M.
PATRICIA SAW RICHARD ACROSS
THE ROOM AND WAS CERTAIN MRS.
JENKINS HAD TURNED HIM GREEN

**PERFORMED BY THE
BARKING PUMPKIN DIGITAL
GRATIFICATION CONSORT
(FRANK ZAPPA, CONDUCTOR)**

FRANCESCO ZAPPA

THE MUSIC OF FRANCESCO ZAPPA (fl. 1763-1788). HIS FIRST DIGITAL RECORDING IN OVER 200 YEARS

FRANCESCO ZAPPA

(ORIGINAL RELEASE: NOVEMBER 1984;
CD RELEASE RYKODISC/RCD 10546)

Frank Zappa was impatient with the 'timeless' sublimity the bourgeoisie profess to find in Bach and Beethoven. The performance of 'dead composer' music is not about musical experience, but show time, a social ritual: 'I find music of the classical period boring because it reminds me of painting by numbers.' declared Zappa. 'All of the norms, as practiced during the olden days, came into being because the guys who paid the bills wanted the tunes they were buying to "sound a certain way". Why is it any better than a bunch of guys in a bar band jamming on "Louie Louie"?'

When Gail Zappa found an entry in the Grove dictionary of music for a certain 'Francesco Zappa' who 'flourished' between 1763 and 1788, Zappa's non-linear imagination was fired. The music was disinterred from the Bancroft Library at Berkeley and the Library of Congress and fed into Zappa's Synclavier. Francesco Zappa is the result. It sounds like a musical Christmas card.

Francesco Zappa is definitely a Zappa release whose value belongs to the, um, conceptual domain. As written down, baroque music is pretty formulaic (there are debates as to how much musicians improvised – or 'embellished' – these scores). Fed into a computer, the music sounds as mechanical as the chimes from a musical box. David Ocker provided hilarious sleevenotes which poked fun at the way the establishment fetishizes the music of the past. Although not phrased in the language of Marx and Freud, these were substantially the same criticisms that Theodor Adorno and Walter Benjamin levelled at the 'timeless' and 'uplifting' art called for by Adolf Hitler. As usual, Zappa's 'jokes' were more perceptive about the conflict between tradition and creativity than the pieties routinely pronounced by the defenders of 'serious music'.). Francesco Zappa also became a character in Zappa's absurdist anti-time book *Them Or Us* (see the bibliography in chapter 11).

ZAPPA

THE YELLOW SHARK
ENSEMBLE MODERN

THE YELLOW SHARK

(ORIGINAL RELEASE: NOVEMBER 1993;
CD RELEASE RYKODISC/RCD 10560)

The Yellow Shark came about when the Ensemble Modern, a contemporary music orchestra based in Frankfurt, asked Zappa to work with them for a season. The musicians flew over to Los Angeles to rehearse. He sampled them for the Synclavier, then used the technology to generate scores. The collaboration led to a series of concerts in Germany in September 1992, which were a resounding success (Zappa proudly included hearty applause between the numbers, a decision regretted by some listeners). The album was first issued by Barking Pumpkin, Zappa's label (when I was up at Laurel Canyon reading Zappa extracts from my *Poodle Play* in late October 1993, Zappa was inspecting the booklet ('too dark?'), and Gail gave me a copy). Rykodisc reproduce the original package: CD in digipack, booklet replete with photographs and notes, all in a brown slipcase.

'Dog Breath Variations' and 'Uncle Meat' reprise the tunes from *Uncle Meat*, turning them into orchestral frolics. 'Outrage At Valdez' was written for a Jacques Cousteau documentary about the Exxon oil-spill in Alaska; a sad melody hovers over tricky meters, producing a mix of mournful sentiment and unease. 'Times Beach' also referred to pollution – a notorious US dioxin disaster – and started life as the 'unplayable' movement in a piece commissioned by the Aspen Wind Quintet. In the notes, conductor Peter Rundel explains how Zappa's sung directions brought out the 'lively' character of a seemingly difficult, abstract score. 'None Of The Above' and 'Ill Revised' derive from a work Zappa wrote for the Kronos String Quartet. 'The Girl In The Magnesium Dress' was a scored version of the Synclavier piece from *The Perfect Stranger*, the Ensemble fully on top of its irrational, Nancarrowish rhythms (in fact, the muscle of their performance gives it a velocity and poise lacking in the earlier version): chimes, piano and marimba stack up stunningly intricate metrics. 'Bebop Tango' (from *Roxy & Elsewhere*) sounds still more circus-like in front of this breathless audience, the tango rhythm introducing the 'difficult' sections as a trombone might usher in an acrobat. 'Food Gathering In Post-Industrial America, 1992' and 'Welcome To The United States' were improvised events designed to foment Zappaesque anarchy (though the applause for Zappa's pro-abortion statement had to be dubbed in). 'Pentagon Afternoon' was, according to Zappa, 'a tone poem – you just have to picture these guys, these dealers in death, sitting around a table in the afternoon in the Pentagon, figuring out what they're going to blow up now, who they're going to subjugate, and what tools they'll use.' It ends in a salvo of plastic ray guns which wipe out the quartet.

Zappa had been performing 'Pound For A Brown' for years, but this was the first time he revealed that it started out as part of a string quartet he wrote in high school 'in 1957 or '58'. 'G-Spot Tornado', an arrangement of the Synclavier piece from *Jazz From Hell* made at the request of the Ensemble, provides a riotous, cossack-kickin' ending. At last, concert musicians had arrived with the rhythmic flair to deal with the demands of the present day composer.

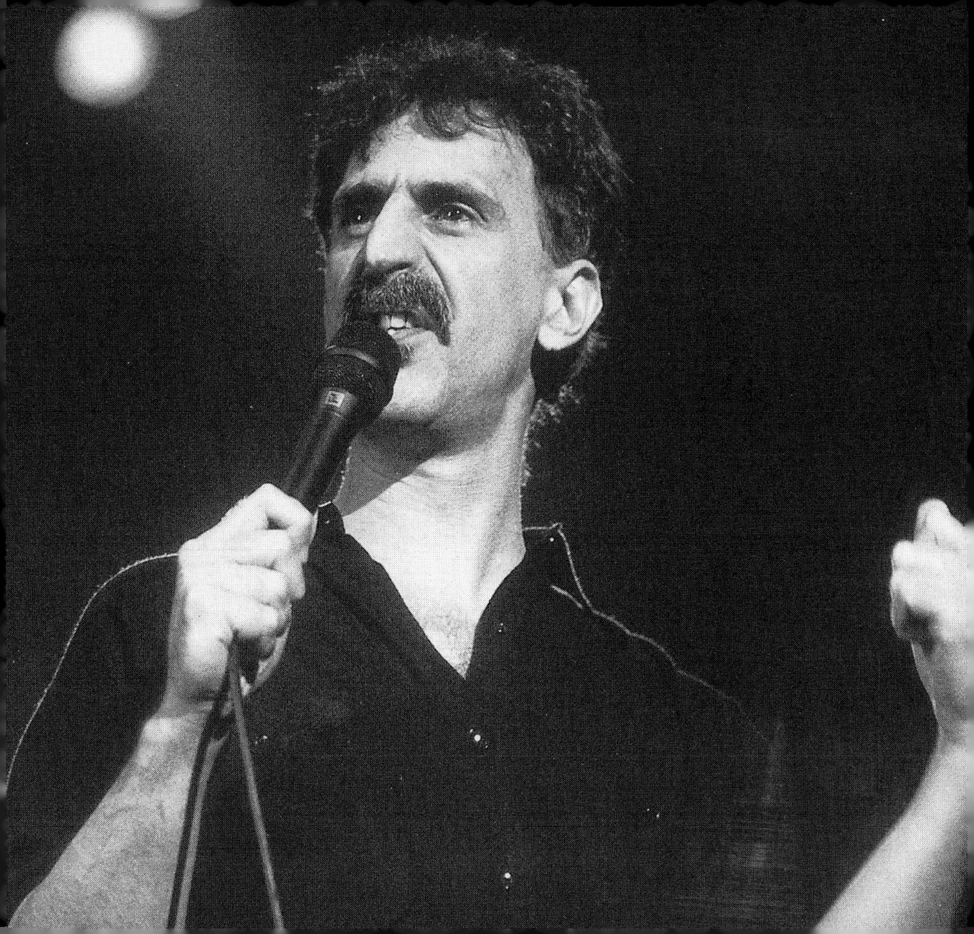

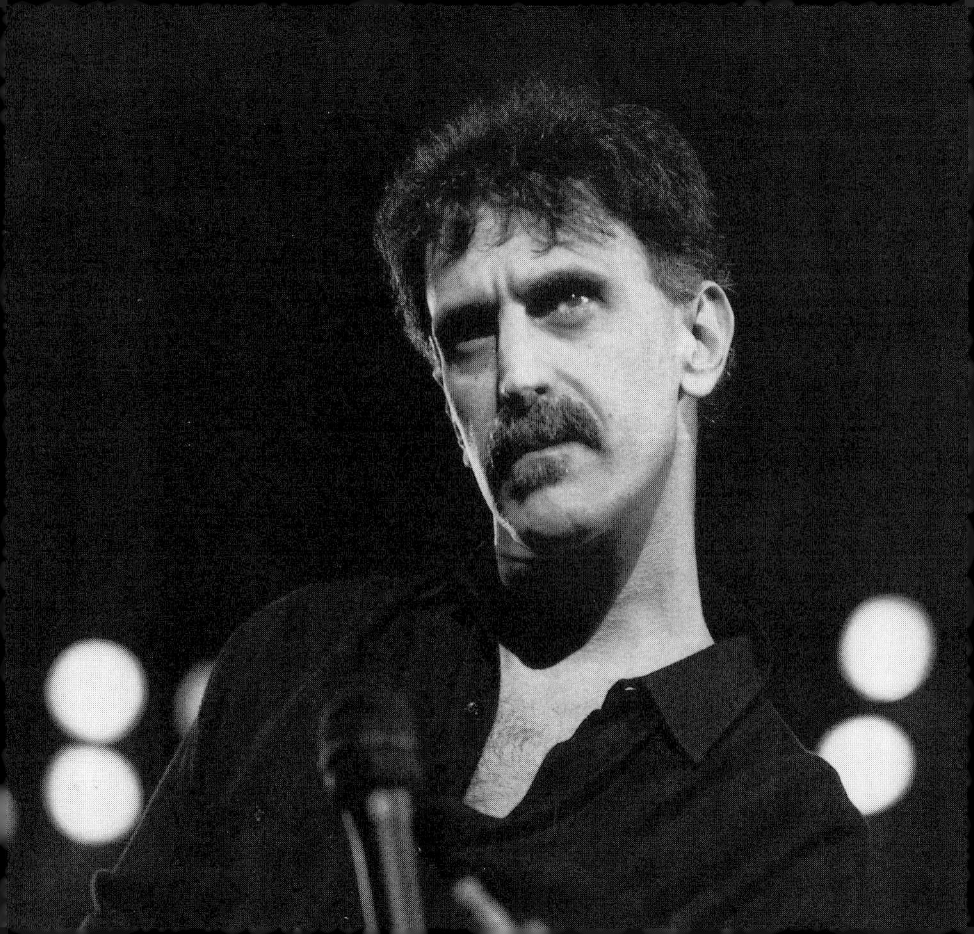

BARKING PUMPKIN

BABY SNAKES

(ORIGINAL RELEASE: MARCH 1983; CD RELEASE RYKODISC/RCD 10539)

Originally released as a mail-order 12" picture-disk in a cellophane sleeve, *Baby Snakes* announced Zappa's latest film: 'a movie about people who do stuff that is not normal'. The title track was the Sheik Yerbouti version of 'Baby Snakes', while the rest – 'Titties & Beer', 'The Black Page #2', 'Jones Crusher', 'Disco Boy', 'Dinah-Moe Humm' and 'Punky's Whips' – came from a concert at the Palladium in New York on 31 October 1977. Personnel details, omitted from the picture-disk, were printed in the Rykodisc CD release, though without instruments (FZ – guitar/vocal; Terry Bozzio – drums/devil vocal; Adrian Belew – guitar/ 'Tiny Lites' vocal; Ed Mann – percussion; Patrick O'Hearn – bass; Tommy Mars – keyboards; Peter Wolf – keyboards). Recording quality is indifferent, and though it's a fine example of the sound and fury of the 1977 band, *Baby Snakes* was more a sign of life than a full-scale album. Fans who want to decipher the mumbled innuendo of 'Disco Boy' on *Zoot Allures* should know that the Rykodisc edition of *Baby Snakes* is the only place they will be able to find a lyric sheet.

ZAPPA
U.M.R.K. DIGITAL REMIX
THEM OR US

THEM OR US

(ORIGINAL RELEASE: DECEMBER 1984;
CD RELEASE RYKODISC/RCD 10543)

If *Baby Snakes* was just a momento of Zappa's film of that name, *Them Or Us* was a full-scale album. The original double-vinyl gatefold was printed on high-gloss card; Donald Roller Wilson's dog Patricia, with her bottle of ketchup and bottle of baby's milk, looked simultaneously cool and crazed (the presence of Patricia connected *Them Or Us* to both *Francesco* and *The Perfect Stranger*; Zappa was also using Wilson's still lifes to decorate his *Old Masters* box sets). The music inside was a devastating onslaught, with outrageous modernist compositions jostling next to scabrous guitar, scurrilous innuendo and just plain madness.

'The Closer You Are' was a cover of an East Coast hit by The Channels. In January 1980, Zappa played the original on BBC Radio One, seguing it into Varèse's 'Hyperprism'. Once you accept the idea that Doo Wop can be as abstract as the most extreme Avant-garde, and that Varèse can be as visceral and moving as rock'n'roll, then the music of *Them Or Us* – indeed all Zappa's music – makes perfect sense. 'In France' showed that Zappa's sojourn in Paris to have his compositions played by the Ensemble InterContemporain had not tempered his gutter humour, and it was particular piquant to hear his original hero Johnny 'Guitar' Watson sing the line 'We cannot wait till we go back, it gets so exciting when the poodles "react"' on 'In France' (this from the man whose own masterpieces included 'Ain't That A Bitch' and 'Bow Wow').

'Ya Hozna' used 'backward-masking' for the entire vocal track, a practice TV Evangelists were claiming was proof that Judas Priest had signed a pact with the Devil. 'Sharleena' revived the song from *Chunga's Revenge* and had Frank's son Dweezil showing how much he had learned from guitarist Eddie Van Halen. 'Sinister Footwear II' and 'Marqueson's Chicken' placed gigantic, jarring guitar in the midst of extraordinarily detailed ensemble passages; 'Truck Driver Divorce' continued the proletarian quandaries of 'No Not Now' (*Drowning Witch*), then dropped the listener into a Zappa-solo battlezone. 'Stevie's Spanking' recounted the exploits of longterm Mothers fan Laurel Fishman, and gave future HM-star Steve Vai and Dweezil opportunity to sound like Halenesque bed-springs. 'Baby, Take Your Teeth Out' pursued the discussion of vagina dentata introduced by 'Jones Crusher' (*Sheik Yerbouti*, *Baby Snakes*) by proposing gummy oral sex. 'Planet Of My Dreams' was another song from the musical 'Hunchentoot' (see *Sleep Dirt*), and 'Be In My Video' mocked pop video clichés (especially David Bowie's 'Let's Dance') with a plethora of silly voices to rival 'Brown Shoes Don't Make It' (*Absolutely Free*) and 'The Radio Is Broken' (*The Man From Utopia*).

'Them Or Us' is a monster of a guitar solo, proving Zappa's assertion that you can swear better on guitar than with words (a trick learned from Johnny 'Guitar' Watson – Zappa was fond of pointing out that Watson could make the guitar say 'son of a bitch!'). 'Frogs With Dirty Little Lips' set words invented by baby Ahmet to a ludicrous march tune. 'Whippin' Post' – the famous fourth side of the Allman Brothers' *Live At The Fillmore* double album – was an opportunity for keyboardist Bobby Martin to vibrate his tonsils and flex his biceps: a rockist counterblast to the afternoons spent watching Pierre Boulez perfect the 'killer triplets' of 'The Perfect Stranger'.

ZAPPA

ORIGINAL CAST RECORDING

THING-FISH

DIGITAL RECORDING

EMI

THING-FISH

(ORIGINAL RELEASE: DECEMBER 1984;
CD RELEASE RYKODISC/RCD 10544/45)

Frank Zappa seemed intent on bankrupting his hardcore fans. Here was a triple-record box set released on the same day as the *Them Or Us* double. There was much dismay about *Thing-Fish*: Zappa was reusing old backing tracks! Terry and Dale Bozzio were all over the record, not drumming or singing, but acting the roles of 'Harry and Rhonda', two yuppie theatre-goers caught in a monstrous musical about potato-headed mammie-nuns, evil princes woofting up potions, rubber-headed sex-aids, crab-grass babies in nativity tableaux and a character called 'Brown Moses' performed by Johnny 'Guitar' Watson. In retrospect, Harry and Rhonda were providing a commentary that pre-echoed the listener's response, a devastatingly disarming device (predicting, incidentally, the strategy of *Beavis & Butthead*, a later favourite of Zappa's).

As to the words spoken by Ike Willis, as the eponymous compère, they... wuz STRICK'LY IN-CROYABLE! Zappa called it a 'negrocious dialect', and said he derived it from Tim Moore's Kingfish character in the TV version of Amos & Andy. With his usual flair for controversy, Zappa had alighted on a topic designed to bring the PC moralist out in a rash (or maybe an epileptic fit). The National Association for the Advancement of Colored People had attacked Moore's character as racist; Zappa simply revelled in Moore's dadaist linguistic 'inventions'.

For Ike Willis, Zappa's wordplay evoked childhood memories: 'in my family, we sort of joke around with dialects, and what it sounded like to me was Paul Laurence Dunbar – he was a black poet from the late nineteenth century who used to write poems in dialects like that... I started giving him copies of Dunbar's work, and eventually that ended up being a big influence on the *Thing-Fish* dialect.' Zappologist Ian Stonehouse connects this fascination with sabotaged lingo to a suppressed tradition of 'artgotique', or mockery of authority; in fact, accusations of 'racism' stem more from people's own snobbish value systems than from Zappa's. It is hard to think that listeners could find a song sung by Johnny 'Guitar' Watson, Ike Willis, Napoleon Murphy Brock and Ray White 'racist' – all singers being both black and highly sensitive to these issues – but many fans simply 'did not wish to know'. Now the truth may be told: *Thing-Fish* is anti-racist satire at the cutting edge, vilifying the 'political correctness' that expresses the condescension of the rich and powerful.

Ike Willis deserved a Grammy for his performance (or perhaps at least a 'Mammie', Miles Davis's suggestion for a non-white-oriented music award). Yet *Thing-Fish* remains undiscovered territory for all but the hardest of hard-core fans. This is a shame, for as Kiwi-based Zappologist Danny Houston discovered when he played 'The Mammy Nuns' on Auckland Radio, this is music of awe-inspiring power and beauty. Thing-Fish's radical deployment of taboo topics never fails to bring changes in the outlook of those exposed – which is practically a definition of the role of real, living Modern Art, folks. As Rhonda says at the end, 'SYMBOLISM! Really deep, intense, thought-provoking Broadway SYMBOLISM. Really Modern, HARRY...'. Amazing.

MEETS THE MOTHERS OF PREVENTION

(ORIGINAL RELEASE: OCTOBER 1985;
CD RELEASE RYKODISC/RCD 10547)

'I Don't Even Care' kicks off *Meets The Mothers Of Prevention* in fine, furious style as Johnny 'Guitar' Watson delivers some characteristic protest lyrics – 'standing in the bread line, everybody line to line, ain't nobody doin' fine... it don't give me no incentive' – over a pleading chorus sung by Ike Willis and Ray White. Unlike *One Size Fits All*, Watson gets to stressify on his guitar strings this time, too. 'One Man, One Vote' demonstrated the intricacies Zappa could achieve on his Synclavier, achieving a humorous, lyrical tone reminiscent of Soft Machine. The title of 'Little Beige Sambo' criticised the new black American middle-class for losing touch with their roots (a point only someone able to deploy a black underground hero like 'Guitar' Watson could pull off). The music is an elaborate fantasy, projecting Conlon Nancarrow's player-piano methodology into stunning perversions. The title of 'Aerobics In Bondage' was a typical Zappa response to Californian inanity. The music likewise: a neo-minimalist, pseudo-ethnic note cycle plunges into harmonic cul-de-sacs and melodic question-marks.

Only one song of Zappa's ever offended guitarist Steve Vai: 'We're Turning Again'. Its vitriol needs to be understood as a protest by someone forever being relegated to 'the sixties' by ignorant journalists. 'Alien Orifice' lives up to its title (those who appreciate the Monkish illusionism of the melody will want to check out the big band version on *Make A Jazz Noise Here*). 'Yo Cats' was directed at the Hollywood session mafia, and 'HR 2911' referred to a House Resolution before Congress in which the record industry proposed to accept censorship in exchange for a tax on blank cassettes.

The epic track on *Meets The Mothers* is 'Porn Wars', which used soundbites from Zappa's testimony at a Congress committee hearing about rock 'obscenity'. Zappa was using the latest technology to make extremely apt points about power, repression and self-serving witch-hunts. Listening on headphones at five o'clock in the morning, composer Simon Fell admitted to being scared; by using samples of the senators themselves (all named in the CD booklet), Zappa brought home the reality of Washington power-mongering (just as the soundbites on *We're Only In It For The Money* revealed the confusions and idiocies of the '60s). The social critic was still firing on all cylinders.

DOES HUMOR BELONG IN MUSIC?

(ORIGINAL RELEASE: JANUARY 1986;
CD RELEASE RYKODISC/RCD 10548)

According to *Frank Zappa – A Visual Documentary* by Miles, Does Humor? was released in Germany and Britain 'without Zappa's permission'. It was mixed and sequenced by him – a selection of tracks from the late-1984 tour – but was not re-released until 1995, sporting a brand new cover by Cal Schenkel (a note inside assures us: 'approved remix and remaster, 1993'). The band at the time consisted of Ike Willis and Ray White (rhythm guitar and vocal), Bobby Martin and Alan Zavod (keyboards), Scott Thunes (bass) and Chad Wackerman (drums). Dweezil Zappa played a solo on 'Whippin' Post'.

As with the *You Can't Do That On Stage Anymore* series, *Does Humor?* is a chance to see how tunes evolved when played by a touring band. 'Tinsel Town Rebellion', for example, has myriad musical embellishments, plus all kinds of ad-libs and lyrical 'transmutations'. Performances are punchy and tidy, usually proceeding at a faster lick than their initial renditions. Formalism has taken grip. The levity with which the singers treat the words indicate that these songs had become vehicles for musicianship: 'Trouble Every Day' and 'What's New In Baltimore' really exist for Zappa's guitar solos. He is superb on the latter, played on 23 December at the Universal Amphitheater in Los Angeles, his last live appearance until the 1988 tour. The inclusion of a 16-minute 'Let's Move To Cleveland' is puzzling: Zappa's guitar solo, recorded at Amherst, starts out-of-tune and sickly but develops some expressive momentum; Alan Zavod and Chad Wackerman contribute nondescript jazz/fusion noodling.

For those who enjoyed the '84 band, *Does Humor?* is a useful momento, but you can't help feeling that while Zappa was onstage he was actually thinking about the latest orchestral project, or simply waiting for his next guitar feature, or the next opportunity to collect some female underwear – or anything 'random' courtesy of lunatics in the audience. But, as he said to Rick Davies in *Music Technology* magazine, 'For today's audience you can't go out and do a whole evening of random behaviour, they're not going to tolerate it, they want to see a structured show. Most people want to have any band go onstage as a human jukebox and just puke out whatever it was they put on a record.' Although he used 'random behaviour' and a vast 'book' of material to avoid stultification, the evidence of *Does Humor?* is that '80s rock shows were not necessarily the best place to catch up with the nonconformist aspects of Zappa's art. Perhaps that's why he stopped touring and turned to the Synclavier.

FRANK ZAPPA
JAZZ FROM HELL

JAZZ FROM HELL

(ORIGINAL RELEASE: NOVEMBER 1986;
CD RELEASE RYKODISC/RCD 10549)

Apart from the track 'St Etienne', all the music on *Jazz From Hell* was programmed on the Synclavier, a digital music-editing suite. Zappa had bought more RAM (random access memory): the bell-like purity of tracks like 'Outside Now Again' on *The Perfect Stranger* has given way to more complex timbres, enabling a more filthy, Zappaesque sound. Given their mode of realisation, it is possible to concentrate on Zappa's compositional predelictions undistracted by considerations of musicianly style and audience expectation. Zappa uses traditional harmonic devices to set up tensions, but resolves them in Chinese-puzzles that rely on mocking repetitions and bizarre shifts of the harmonic environment around the solo 'line'. New-music magazine *The Wire* was impressed: 'With *Jazz From Hell*, Zappa leaps to the top of the list of world-class futuro-composers'.

Zappa-biographer Michael Gray found *The Wire*'s 'gush' exaggerated, arguing that *Jazz From Hell* 'sounds unsurprisingly like a bunch of Zappa's musicians having a normal day – actually rather a dreary day – on which we're grateful for the absence of vocals nudge-nudging their way through lyrics to suit the spiritual needs of an imaginary 13-year-old boy.' This fails to register the peculiar claustrophobia and poignancy of the record. 'St Etienne' – a lyrical Zappa guitar outing with the 1981 touring band, played in real time – made the rest of the record sound still more tinny and mechanical. Like Miles Davis's contemporary *Tutu* – also realised on the Synclavier – the record has an ersatz feel that it was possible to miss when the technology was brand new.

Though Gray will doubtless demur, it was precisely Zappa's ability to deal with the ersatz that was his forté. From the 'trivial poop' of 'Motherly Love' (*Freak Out!*) to 'Bogus Pomp' (*London Symphony Orchestra*), Zappa's art thrives on ambivalence. Heard this way, *Jazz From Hell*'s 'ersatz' quality becomes a remarkable meditation on the nature of 'free' expression. Zappa announced that the Synclavier would free him of dependence on musicians, yet when he comes to expressing his unalloyed personal soul, it is a compendium of nostalgic memories: Jean-Luc Ponty's violin tone ('Night School'), Art Tripp's percussion ('The Beltway Bandits'), Ruth Underwood's marimba ('While You Were Art II'), Art Barrow's syncopated bass plucks ('G-Spot Tornado'). In an interview, Zappa mentioned that a machine wouldn't crack him up by ad-libbing 'Hi Ho Silver'; a sample of Ike Willis's favourite onstage interjection swims through the mix of 'Massaggio Galore', like a trapped spirit gabbling in the swirl of a Hollywood horror effect. Zappa's anti-musician, anti-union rhetoric notwithstanding, he was too conscientious an artist not to express the truth of his materials, and the melancholy, fidgetting, constrained tone of these Synclavier pieces speaks volumes about the difference between individual and collective freedom.

FRANK ZAPPA · GUITAR

GUITAR

(ORIGINAL RELEASE: APRIL 1988;
CD RELEASE RYKODISC/RCD 1050/51)

On *Shut Up 'N' Play Your Guitar*, John Swenson's sleevenote warned that the album was but 'the tip of the iceberg'; in April 1988 Zappa released 19 guitar solos in a 2-record album on his own Barking Pumpkin label, while Rykodisc issued a 2-CD album containing 32 solos. It became obvious that Zappa, with his famous hoard of unreleased material, was looking forward to a CD future. Production values had improved: though some missed Vinnie Colaiuta's rhythmic empathy, others were impressed by the sculptural majesty of the mix.

One of the oddest things about *Guitar* was the opener, 'Sexual Harassment In The Workplace', a straight blues – which Zappa always said was too constricting for him, like 'wearing tight shoes'. However, after this perverse declaration of 'normality', things become more rhythmically strange and rigorous as Zappa set his soloistic anomalies against the tightest bass/drums team he'd ever employed (apart from 'Outside Now (Original Solo)' and 'Systems Of Edges' from 1979, all tracks came from 80s ensembles with the Scott Thunes/Chad Wackermann rhythm section). Zappa once said of Elmore James that to the unpractised ear 'it all sounds the same', but that once you get into his sound, there's a world there. The same goes for *Guitar*. Zappa's combination of power and melancholy, the sense of huge event underpinned by yearning unease, sets a pretty unvaried emotional 'tone' (the vocal 'blips' that separated the tracks of *Shut Up* are absent). However, if the music is approached 'statistically', rather than merely for how it sounds, there is both conscientious detail and startling invention.

FRANK ZAPPA

BROADWAY THE HARD WAY

BROADWAY THE HARD WAY

(ORIGINAL RELEASE: OCTOBER 1988;
CD RELEASE RYKODISC/RCD 1052)

In 1988, Zappa emerged from behind his Synclavier. After four months rehearsal, an eleven-piece band was ready for a world tour. *Broadway The Hard Way* presented the new songs, an intricate studio weave of recordings made during a total of 85 performances. The record is a grand statement about the state of modern America. Zappa posed in a mock-up of the presidential suite, his hair standing on end and Ronald Reagan's notorious quote – 'facts are stupid things' – sprayed on the wall. Eagle-eyed continuity-sleuths noted that the slogan on the back of his copy of *Soldier Of Fortune* read 'the party's over'. Zappa saw Christian-Right Fundamentalism as the new Fascism, and his tour was a stand against it.

Superficially, 'Elvis Has Just Left The Building' is a typical Zappa put-down, but it was really Zappa bidding adieu to rock'n'roll. The music on *Broadway The Hard Way* harks back to jazz, to cabaret, to TV theme-music, to hymns, to electioneering razzamatazz, but there is nothing one can call 'rock'. 'Planet Of The Baritone Women', Zappa insisted, was about stock-exchange yuppies – ie men – but it's hard to square that with the lyrics. 'Any Kind Of Pain' voices Zappa's thoughts as he watches TV, staring at the PR bimbos who soft-sell big-business policies to the American public. 'Dickie's Such An Asshole', the tune from the *Roxy & Elsewhere* era, was a dark reminder of Richard Nixon and the failings of the American electoral process: 'There's just one thing I wanna know – how'd that asshole ever manage to get in?'.

There's a desperation to 'When The Lie's So Big', as if Zappa's commitment to honesty and reason cannot credit the gangsterism of modern American politics. 'Rhymin' Man' shows that Zappa put little faith in the Democrats either. 'Stolen Moments' from Oliver Nelson's 1961 classic *Blues And The Abstract*

Truth (with Eric Dolphy) features a beautiful trumpet solo by Walt Fowler. 'Murder By Numbers' brought Sting on stage to complain about TV Evangelists who claimed the devil had written the tune ('I wrote the fucking song!'); A&M let Sting appear on the record provided Zappa's publicity kept quiet about it. 'Jezebel Boy' is a Chandleresque tale of ruling-class sexual hypocrisy, a follow-up to 'Idiot Bastard Son' (*We're Only In It For The Money*) and 'Teenage Prostitute' (*Drowning Witch*). 'Jesus Thinks You're A Jerk' was a diatribe versus Jimmy Swaggart, TV Evangelist and Jerry Lee Lewis's cousin, latest news of whose downfall was gleefully announced at Zappa's performance at the Brighton Conference Centre on 16 April 1988 (thus brightening an unpleasant reminder of 70s arena-rock 'culture', with overflowing urinals and no pass-outs at intermission). *Broadway The Hard Way* was Zappa's last public 'statement': as unreconciled with America's establishment as ever.

THE BEST BAND YOU NEVER HEARD IN YOUR LIFE

(ORIGINAL RELEASE: MARCH 1991;
CD RELEASE RYKODISC/RCD 1053/54)

Like many veteran leaders, Zappa delegated authority. In the 1988 band, bassist Scott Thunes was in charge of rehearsals. Band members objected to his manner ('abrasive, blunt and rude', according to Miles). In June, Zappa told a mutinying crew that he had ten weeks of bookings in America, and asked them if they'd carry on with Thunes – all of them (apart from Mike Keneally, a longterm Zappa fan before graduating to bandmember) refused. Rather than replace Thunes and give in to the musicians, Zappa cancelled the tour and took a big loss. Never someone to protect his audience from the grim realities of musical production, Zappa named the album for fans deprived of their gigs. First released as a double-CD on Zappa Records, Rykodisc replaced the original cover (a dull, uncredited photograph of the band on stage) with nifty artwork by Cal Schenkel.

Best Band comprises old songs and covers of famous rock tunes. Everything benefits from the five-man horn section of Walt Fowler (trumpet), Bruce Fowler (trombone), Paul Carman, Albert Wing and Kurt McGettrick (saxes), a juicy ebullience unheard since the Brecker brothers played on *Zappa In New York*. 'Bolero' is muscular and tightly organized, compressing Ravel into a gleaming chunk of saxophone reggae. Disc one concludes with 'Mr Green Genes' and a suite from *One Size Fits All*. Though these versions lack the textural contrasts of the studio original, live rendition gives them a special thrust.

Disc two begins with 'Purple Haze' in Devo style, one of the generic beats – ska, reggae, heavy-metal, Weather-Report – Zappa cued with hand signals. 'A Few Moments With Brother A. West' has the graphic designer for *The Real Frank Zappa Book* and *Broadway The Hard Way* make a satirical rightwing speech – he did it with such conviction that Zappa had to assure his audience that he was not for real in order to secure his safety after the show. The album ends in a series of songs altered to knock TV Jimmy Swaggart. This kind of tomfoolery is typical of Zappa's instinct for the perverse: he spent four months rehearsing this band to play an extravagantly wide selection of his songs with unerring accuracy, and then releases takes which feature on-the-spot changes. 'The Eric Dolphy Memorial Barbecue' exploits the jazz sleaze of the horns: Paul Carman revives some of Eric Dolphy's alto licks, while Walt Fowler is beautifully sleek and burnished. An appearance of 'The Blue Danube' was a salute to Vienna, one of the sites for its recording.

ZAPPA'S
MAKE A JAZZ NOISE HERE

MAKE A JAZZ NOISE HERE

(ORIGINAL RELEASE: MAY 1991;
CD RELEASE RYKODISC/RCD 1055/56)

Make A Jazz Noise Here collected together the more outlandish instrumentals from the 1988 tour. Although only three tracks were première recordings, plentiful solos and collective improvisations make this much more than a live album of cover versions. The title was explained by Zappa to Den Simms: 'You ever heard of Erroll Garner, jazz pianist, who mumbles along with what he plays? "Ayee! Ayee!" It's the whole concept of jazz musicians who make jazz noises while they perform.'

'When Yuppies Go To Hell' is a free-form collage that recalls *Weasels*. Sections run the gamut from belch samples (courtesy Zappa's nephew Jade) to Webern-like purity, from funk bass to jew's harp and Hammond organ: dada cabaret. 'Fire and Chains' is a guitar solo, sampled guitar loops achieving a denser texture than those on *Guitar*. The band gallop through some themes from *Money*, *Weasels* and *Lumpy Gravy*, showing how far from rock and how close to Broadway these tunes actually were. Mike Keneally's evocation of George Duke's funky intro to 'Eat That Question' is beautifully unpressured and soulful. Trumpeter Walt Fowler takes his time, providing a special gleaming lyricism that keeps grabbing one's attention with the '88 band.

In the 1988 arrangement, 'Big Swifty' combines the gorgeous big band sound of the Wazoo band with the rock drive of the 80s; the solos quote from such classical pops as Wagner's *Lohengrin* and Tchaikovsky's *1812 Overture*, while a fully-arranged crowdpleaser has the entire brass section play music from Bizet's *Carmen*. What is refreshing about the music of *Jazz Noise* is that it can plunder jazz for flexibility and response without adopting the vacuous virtuosity of fusion. The gruelling repetitions of Zappa's tours in the '80s, the joyless run-throughs of anti-rock and cul-de-sac pop, suddenly evaporate into music as creatively interactive as it is funny and unpretentious.

Disc two of *Jazz Noise* begins with a 'New Age' version of 'The Black Page'. Originally written to exact creative hysteria from Terry Bozzio, in the hands of these musicians it becomes a tender ballad. 'Dupree's Paradise' could have been written for this horn-rich line-up, and features wonderful trumpet from Fowler. 'City Of Tiny Lites' gains a crunching bass riff courtesy Kurt McGettrick's baritone sax. Against a steady clave beat Zappa's guitar sounds peculiarly robust and rugged. On the tour, mixer Harry Andronis (who had attended every Zappa tour since 1973 and always taken exception to what he considered excessive amounts of mixing-desk effects) kept the sound natural.

The sudden eruption of 'Stevie Spanking' in all this complexity is a reminder of the incongruity that makes Zappa's music thought-provoking. 'Alien Orifice' again benefits from the horn section; Chad Wackerman's drumming is particularly responsive on the solo, full of strange gaps and sudden cymbal enthusiasms. 'Cruisin' For Burgers' sees Zappa unfurl one of his great pieces of claustrophobic lyricism, a solo that consists of one long melody.

The cover of *Jazz Noise* shows a nightclub named 'Zappa's' built over still-combusting industrial waste: a sign reads: 'last chance for live music'. *Jazz Noise* documents the wildest and most speculative music that has been heard in rock arenas since the days of Cream, Hendrix and the Mothers Of Invention.

DIGGING THE ARCHIVE

YOU CAN'T DO THAT ON STAGE ANYMORE VOL. 1

(ORIGINAL RELEASE: APRIL 1988; RYKODISC/RCD10561/62)

Following his perception that linear time is an 'affliction', Zappa did not issue his archive of live recordings in any kind of chronological order. Matt Groening reports that Zappa looked horrified at his suggestion that he release entire concerts by particular bands: 'That's the kind of thing bootleggers do!'. So the *Stage* series segues performances from different eras, and in a bravura edit – using a new digital device called Sonic Solutions – Zappa welded a version of 'Lonesome Cowboy Burt' from 1971 into one from 1988. These twelve CDs present an 'ideal' Zappa concert that draws from two decades worth of material – 1968 to 1988.

Vol.1 begins with band banter at Florida Airport, as Volman and Kaylan exchange pleasantries about puking on stage. 'He saved it because he might be hungry later,' says Zappa. It is hard not to interpret this as Zappa's comment on his own habit of hoarding so many old performances on tape. 'Get the big pieces!' says Volman. The Stage series includes some very big pieces indeed.

Vol.1 is sandwiched between two versions of 'Sofa' and includes the famous matinée performance at Hammersmith Odeon where 'Don't Eat The Yellow Snow' became the occasion for mass poetry recitation (and for Zappa to show off his knowledge of *Under Milk Wood*). There are three songs from an MTV concert special: after the banning of his 'You Are What You Is' video, Zappa thought it 'unlikely that they'll ever let us get away with that again'.

YOU CAN'T DO THAT ON STAGE ANYMORE VOL.2

(ORIGINAL RELEASE: OCTOBER 1988; RYKODISC/RCD10563/64)

Vol.2 is the only one in the Stage series to accede to Matt Groening's request for a whole concert. It memorialises a band of which Zappa was especially fond, usually referred to as the Roxy band: Napoleon Murphy Brock on sax and vocals, George Duke on keyboards, Ruth Underwood on percussion, Tom Fowler on bass and Chester Thompson on drums. It was recorded at Helsinki in Finland on 22 September 1974. It's brilliant!

YOU CAN'T DO THAT ON STAGE ANYMORE VOL.3

(ORIGINAL RELEASE: NOVEMBER 1989; RYKODISC/RCD10565/66)

Disc one is devoted to performances by Zappa's 1984 touring band. 'Drowning Witch' is merged with a 1982 version because, according to Zappa, 'the 1984 band never played it correctly during its 6-month tour, and the 1982 band only managed to get close on one occasion'. Disc two includes 'Dickie's Such An Asshole', the song for President Richard Nixon; Terry Bozzio's demonstration of the virtues of 'real' drums; a merger of two versions of 'Zoot Allures', from Japan and France; a sequence of songs from *You Are What You Is* broadcast on MTV and a marathon 'King Kong' splicing together versions from 1971 and 1982.

YOU CAN'T DO THAT ON STAGE ANYMORE VOL.4

(ORIGINAL RELEASE: MAY 1991; RYKODISC/RCD10567/68)

Disc one has seven songs from the 1984 tour, two from 1988 and one each from 1969, 1976, 1978, 1979, 1980 and 1982. Standout tracks are a 1973/1984 collage of 'Montana' and the 'original' 'The Torture Never Stops', where Captain Beefheart's vocal and a stomping 'Smokestack Lightnin'' riff make it sound utterly different from its final form on *Zoot Allures*. Disc two has seven songs from 1984 and six from 1982.

For this listener, Stage's emphasis on live rock material from the 80s is a disadvantage, because the musicians are so proficient and disciplined, versions are not substantially different: 'Advance Romance', a swaggering blues work-out on *Bongo Fury*, full of character and humour, has become such a set piece that the versions on Vol.3 (1984 band) and Vol.5 (1982 band) clock in with only three seconds difference. For a seven-minute tune recorded two years apart, the control is awe-inspiring, but mere tightness does not necessarily make for an inspiring listen.

YOU CAN'T DO THAT ON STAGE ANYMORE VOL.5

(ORIGINAL RELEASE: AUGUST 1992; RYKODISC/RCD10569/70)

Disc one covers the years 1965 to 1969 'specifically for the amusement of those collectors who still believe that the only "good" material was performed by those early line-ups' and is a collection of avantgarde tunes and 'bus' recordings that will delight fans of the original Mothers. Disc two is the 1982 band, culled from Geneva, Munich, Balzano and Frankfurt and will delight people who liked that band.

YOU CAN'T DO THAT ON STAGE ANYMORE VOL.6

(ORIGINAL RELEASE: AUGUST 1992; RYKODISC/RCD10571/72)

Disc one collects together Zappa's songs 'dealing generally with the topic of sex' and has variety, shock and spunk aplenty (on 'Wind Up Workin' In A Gas Station', there is a rare chance to hear singer Bianca Thornton). Disc two has many tunes from Zappa's Halloween shows at the Palladium in New York, where the crowd's hysteria creates a special atmosphere. It all ends with a magnificent 'Strictly Genteel' from 1981, Zappa's secular blessing providing a suitable finish to his entire monstrous project.

Frank Zappa
PLAYGROUND PSYCHOTICS
THE MOTHERS OF INVENTION
FILLMORE EAST N.Y.C.
PAULEY PAVILION UCLA
RAINBOW THEATER LONDON

PLAYGROUND PSYCHOTICS

(ORIGINAL RELEASE: OCTOBER 1992; RYKODISC/RCD 10557/58)

According to Zappa, *Playground Psychotics* went 'beyond mere rock'n'roll into the dangerous realm of social anthropology'. His habit of taping players offstage was notorious, and provided a memorable scene in *200 Motels*, where Mark Volman and Howard Kaylan explain that he listens to the band in order to steal material to give back to them to play in the movie. 'The London Cabtape' creates a vertiginous hall of mirrors as we hear Zappa, Aynsley Dunbar and Volman listening to the latter's own tape-recording of Kaylan, Simmons and Underwood planning a revolt against Zappa's rule. 'It's A Good Thing We Get Paid To Do This' is Volman's 'bootleg' recording of a rehearsal; bandmembers found themselves reading scripts Zappa has transcribed from their own taped statements – complaining about how he does just that!

As well as such paranoid-critical games with tape-recorders, there's some excellent music: songs from *We're Only In It For The Money* and *Uncle Meat* performed by the Fillmore East band, and a clearly-mixed version of the Fillmore East jam with John and Yoko previously released on Lennon's *Some Time In New York City* album. There is a thirty-minute alternate performance of 'Billy Mountain' from *Just Another Band From LA*, and selections of dialogue from the video *The True Story Of 200 Motels*. *Playground Psychotics* is paradise for Zappa obsessives and anyone interested in speculation about representation, power and the status of 'the real' – and probably hell for everybody else (though this author is long past second-guessing the responses of the latter constituency).

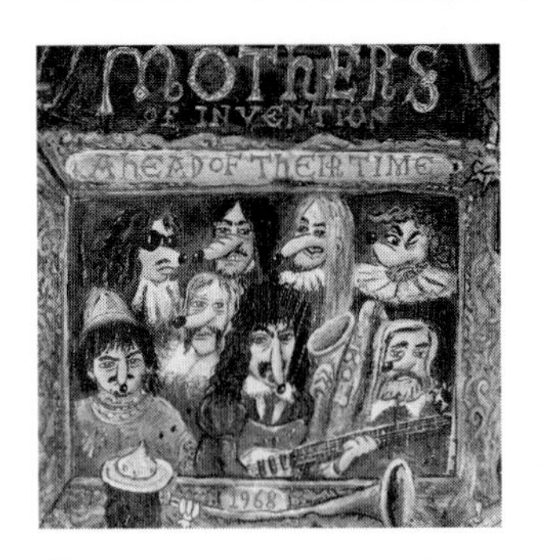

AHEAD OF THEIR TIME

(FIRST RELEASE: MARCH 1993 RYKODISC/RCD 10559)

Ahead Of Their Time is the concert performed by the Mothers Of Invention at the Royal Albert Hall on 28 October 1968. It supplied a few bars for 'Prelude To The Afternoon Of A Sexually Aroused Gas Mask' and 'The Orange County Lumber Jack' on Weasels Ripped My Flesh, but is mainly unheard material. It was something of a deluxe concert, with fourteen members of the BBC Symphony Orchestra playing Zappa's scores, and scripted dialogue by the Mothers: a sketch for the 'rock versus classical'/'life versus art' confrontations that propel 200 Motels. Roy Estrada's 'Mexican' pleading must be heard to be believed!

In his note, Zappa complains about hiss supplied by Don Preston's keyboard set-up, but the sound is solid and clear. 'King Kong', 'Transyvania Boogie' and a ten-minute work-out on 'The Orange County Lumber Track': though this ensemble lacks the suave ferocity of Zappa's later bands, it has a clunking forthrightness that never fails to charm. Cal Schenkel's time-warp cover art – dated, like the cosmic sofa of *One Size Fits All*, to the seventeenth century – folds out into a magnificent panoply of conceptual-continuity motifs.

THE LOST EPISODES

(FIRST RELEASE: FEBRUARY 1996 RYKODISC/RCD 40573)

Studio outtakes, from The Blackouts – a teenage R&B combo in which Zappa played drums, and which supported Earl Bostic and Louis Armstrong at the Shrine Auditorium for a NAACP benefit in the late '50s – through to the version of 'I Don't Wanna Get Drafted' that was issued as an anti-war single in 1980. According to engineer Spence Chrislu, *The Lost Episodes* was 'tribute to his fans, a sort of dropping the veil and just saying, "this is what went on behind the scenes, and here are some explanations, here's some fun stuff that never made it anywhere else – and this is for you guys".'

'Lost In A Whirlpool' is Captain Beefheart in 1959, singing about being flushed down the toilet, with Zappa on lead and his brother Bobby on rhythm guitar. Ronnie and Kenny tell the story of the nasal excavations described in 'Let's Make The Water Turn Black' on *We're Only In It For The Money*. 'Mount St Mary's Concert' (1963) is two minutes from Zappa's pre-rock period – avantgarde classical with laughs. 'Take Your Clothes Off When You Dance' is a Zappa melody played by jazz professionals at Paul Buff's studio in 1961. 'Handsome Cabin Boy' is a Ewan MacColl sea-shanty played by the Mothers. Ricky Lancelotti sings 'Wonderful Wino'; Sugarcane Harris sings 'Sharleena' and plays violin on an instrumental called 'Lil' Clanton Shuffle'. An early instrumental version of 'Inca Roads' by the Overnite Sensation band. Zappa's Luden's Cough Drop commercial from 1967. Captain Beefheart reads the original 'Wazoo' backed by a Synclavier track. Zappa jams with the *Trout Mask* Magic Band...

All this and detailed, painstaking notes by Rip Rense with quotes from Frank, Captain Beefheart, Ruth Underwood and Terry Bozzio. If you're not already rushing down to the record shop, then don't bother – you're not a Zappa fan (yet).

HAVE I OFFENDED SOMEONE?

(FIRST RELEASE: APRIL 1997 RYKODISC/RCD 10577)

The idea of a collection of all Zappa's most 'offensive' material hardly seemed the right way to go about preserving his legacy. However, unlike the Rykodisc collections *Strictly Commercial* and *Strictly Genteel, Have I Offended Someone*? was compiled and segued by Zappa. In the midst of the adulations he was receiving – *The Yellow Shark, BBC Late Show* arts documentaries – he wanted to remind everyone of the way he refused to kowtow to PC rules.

His remixes make the grooves more succulent and compatible: 'Goblin Girl', for example, is slowed down and 'Dinah-Moe Humm' has all kinds of sweaty embellishments, with George Duke funky keyboards well to the fore during a more realistically-timed orgasm (the appearance of some lines from 'Montana' at a crucial point had poodle-play scholars scurrying for their typewriters). Well, was Zappa anti-semitic, anti-gay, and sexist as some obituarists argued? No. Quite the opposite, in fact. It points to the conformist and cowardly nature of identity politics, that someone as resolutely critical of the establishment as Zappa should be pilloried in the name of progressive ideas. Zappa's outsider status in a 'culture' designed to apply a liberal gloss to the needs of the almighty dollar meant challenging the listener to rise above petty correctness. This is a Soundtrack for the Enlightened: for those who can see that it is censorious Christian-right fundamentalists who are the Fascists, not those who laugh when the lust and anguish boiling beneath the surface of respectability spew forth in lurid satirical ditties.

As Ed Sanders of The Fugs points out in his essay in the accompanying booklet: 'What gives *Have I Offended Someone*? its fine power to arouse and even offend is the strength and complex precision of the performances, the editing and mixing, and the brilliance of the compositions...

Zappa was a brilliant rhapsodist, as in the Ancient Greek sense: a singer who "stitches together" fragments from a variety of sources to form a work.'

Despite complaints from predictable quarters, the final impression made by *Have I Offended Someone?* is the skill and flexibility of Zappa's art: even in his 'stupid' songs the variety and unexpectedness of his musical juxtapositions still astonish.

FRANK ZAPPA
CIVILIZATION PHAZE III

THE FINAL MASTERPIECE

CIVILIZATION PHAZE III

(FIRST RELEASE: DECEMBER 1994 ZAPPA RECORDS CDDZAP 56)

Frank Zappa's art refuses safe niches. It proceeds by asking questions. To gauge something as mighty as the two-CD *Phaze III*, you need to step back a little, take in some historical perspective. After all, Zappa was dealing with civilisation on the grand scale here (though of course he spelt it with a 'z'...).

After World War II, serialism – Schoenberg and Webern's upturning of the whole edifice of western music – became an orthodoxy: as long as composers accepted the state-funded art niche, serialist 'innovation' and 'experiment' were fine. Post-war Modern Art was the badge of a new, rational, UN-approved world order supposedly totally different from the regimes of Hitler and Stalin. Stockhausen and Boulez were the musical equivalents of the lab-coated technicians who were splitting the atom to create a future of cheap electricity, chrome, rubber and household tidiness. In America, Milton Babbitt founded a school of what Zappa called 'boop-beep'. Though Babbitt's music itself is dazzling, academia insulated avantgarde composition from the public, preventing it from asking awkward questions about the limits of freedom and dissent in a consumer society.

Zappa's oeuvre was one long interrogation of what constitutes musical 'value' and what constitutes 'freedom'. Always on a knife-edge between technical excellence and rubbishing non-seriousness, his music offends rock apologists because of its sceptical attitude towards pop (see Lester Bangs, Chuck Eddy, Ian Penman). However, if you pare away the myths and politics and verbiage and take a hard look at its musical content, pop and rock do emerge as incredibly limited. Anyone who has understood and loved the music of, say, Stravinsky and Nono,

Mingus and Dolphy, must find a diet of 'Louie Louie' absurd.

Zappa's absurdism allowed him to indulge the joys of the utterly crass – he was sincere when he called Black Sabbath's 'Iron Man' a classic – as much as it allowed him to disengage advanced music from snobbism and intellectualist intimidation. Some listeners regret the segue of 'Black Page #2' into 'Big Leg Emma' on *Zappa In New York*, but that's the whole point: rather than pretending to heal splits in the social psyche via middle-of-the-road compromise, Zappa dramatises them by pursuing them to extremes.

Civilization Phaze III was Zappa's last great work, consciously fashioned as such as he succumbed to prostate cancer. The Synclavier and work with the Ensemble Modern gave him access to a fantastic orchestral palette. His perverse rhythmic ideas could now be carried out faultlessly; the instrumental sounds were glowingly true. Given all this power and freedom, it might be assumed that Zappa would create a towering, substantial masterpiece. However, he was far too aware of the social implications of 'art' music to do anything so positivist. He was also too aware of the technical problems of modern music to believe that a new vocabulary can simply be plucked from the air.

Zappa's musical credo was 'If it sounds good to you, it's bitchen; and if it sound bad to you, it's shitty': that is the organising 'principle' behind the music on *Civilization Phaze III*. Melancholy woodwind and string sounds are prominent, the opposite of the guitar/brass brashness that characterizes rock and soul. However, these classical sonorities never congeal into a style. They continually disperse into uncertainty and quandary. There are rhythmic progressions that lift off from Conlon Nancarrow's concept of superimposed, 'xenochronous' time-signatures, but the technique never becomes dogma. Zappa listens in to the emotional effect of his experiments, and then responds with intuitive breaks, jokes and segues. These will be as incomprehensible to literal-minded ('Schenkerian') analysis as the improvised transgressions of late Beethoven or the 'free' atonality of early Schoenberg.

Phaze III has spoken-word interludes between each piece of music. When Zappa played me disc two of *Civilization Phaze III* in his living room, we were frequently diverted into conversation, but whenever the voices started up, he would shush me into listening. These bizarre dialogues were of great importance to him. Some contend that *Phaze III* would be better 'without the voices', but this misapprehends Zappa's intentions as grossly as the DJs who wished he'd just produce 'viable rock'n'roll' and stop 'sabotaging' his own efforts. As he said to Dan Forte, 'maybe the sabotage is the actual information in the song'.

The spoken-word interludes splice together recordings made in 1967 with recordings made in 1991. In both sessions, people were placed inside a piano and encouraged to speculate about music and society. With characteristic prescience, Zappa selected the Ensemble Modern's Hermann Kretzschmar to represent the land of Mozart and recording technology: it was a Wendell Kretschmar's lectures on Beethoven that spurred the hero of Thomas Mann's *Doctor Faustus* to become a composer (this novel, with its discussions of teeth, Nazism and the possibility of a populist avantgarde could have been the blueprint for Zappa's oeuvre). Note the spookily-appropriate addition of the 'z' to his name! Meanwhile, actor Michael Rappaport praises Rap (Niggaz With Attitude, Public Enemy, Brand Nubians) and Ali Asken talks Turkish (which annoys Rappaport). As usual, Zappa's music is the terrain for an encounter between different cultures, and raises the utopian dream of a universal human language (Tuvan throat singing haunts 'Beat The Reaper'). 'Dio Fa' is an orchestral *étude*, but its use of drum and bass predicts the junglist drum'n'bass of, say, Roni Size Reprazent: Zappa's rhythmic impetus is American, and so rooted in Africa.

Civilization Phaze III is a complex and vivid dialogue about modern music. Its quandaries are the driving force of its compositions. Spider concludes by saying 'our strength comes from our uncertainty, if we understood music we'd be bored with it'. This goes with Zappa's 'the universe works whether or not we understand it': for him, consolation is not to be found in ideas or philosophy or faiths, but in restless curiosity about the actual, material world. Zappa was an anti-authoritarian materialist in the tradition of Giordano Bruno and Josef Dietzgen. *Phaze III* finishes with 'Waffenspiel' ('weapon play' in German), a recording of home-owners in the San Fernando Valley shooting their automatic weapons skyward at New Year in 1987. What should be celebratory fireworks has become a manifestation of property-owner paranoia and aggression. The pained expression on Zappa's face as he described these 'assholes' said everything about his art's relation to society: his music was always objective investigation, a telling of home truths.

APPENDIX

COLLECTABLES/ODDITIES

In the years Zappa's back catalogue was out of print, second-hand prices of his original records soared to the £50 mark. Now that Rykodisc has the whole oeuvre available in conscientously repackaged CDs – often with extra tracks and artwork – the prices of the original vinyl has stabilised, and in some cases fallen.

Vinyl 7" singles by Zappa are highly prized. Novelty singles cut with Paul Buff and Ray Collins at PAL Studios (later Studio Z) on the Original Sound label are now as rare as the proverbial hen's teeth, likewise 'How Could I Be Such A Fool?', 'Who Are The Brain Police?' and 'Why Don't You Do Me Right' b/w 'Big Leg Emma' on Verve. Throughout his career, a single was usually issued to go with an album, but on the rare occasions singles were played on the radio, the audience's response was to buy the album rather than the single anyway. The popularity of *Sheik Yerbouti* in continental Europe spawned some hits, so that 'Bobby Brown' and 'Stick It Out' may be obtained as singles in Scandinavia and Germany. Because it was issued as a single with a 'message' (and a great pic-sleeve by Cal Schenkel), 'I Don't Wanna Get Drafted' is worth obtaining. 'Valley Girl' was a bona fide hit, so copies of this are worthwhile.

Some collectors go for 12" vinyl singles. Ones to look out for: 'Dancin' Fool', with a fine portrait à la *Sheik Yerbouti*, with a tarbooshed Zappa smoking a Winston through a cigarette holder, and some extra breaks edited in to make the song 'disco' length; 'True Glove', with Zappa fisting an oven glove, and a backwards version of 'No Not Now' called 'Won Ton On' with Johnny 'Guitar' Watson's verbal ejactament a (rather than Harry & Rhonda's, as on *Thing-Fish*); Zappa's interview picture disc from *Talking Pictures*, the 'Valley Girl' with a touching father/daughter photo on the cover; and finally 'Stairway To Heaven' with its satirical, anti-transcendent image of fire-escapes leading nowhere.

In 1969, Zappa and Herbie Cohen founded two labels, Straight and Bizarre. Some fascinating records resulted. *Trout Mask Replica* [Warner/Reprise 2027] by Captain Beefheart and the Magic Band is acknowledged as a classic (John Peel recently named it as his favourite rock record of all time). No self-respecting Zappaphile should persist without a copy. Luckily it's out on CD (with a lyric-sheet, a luxury denied original purchasers). *An Evening With Wild Man Fischer* was a double album 'documenting' an eccentric who sold songs for a dime on the streets of Hollywood: by turns funny, insightful and scary. A CD version of *Permanent Damage* by The GTO's appeared briefly, but is now almost as rare as the vinyl: this collection of songs and statements by a gang of groupies (with contributions by Lowell George, Don Preston, Rod Stewart and Jeff Beck) is a favourite among Zappa cognoscenti (punk principles notwithstanding, cartoonist Savage Pencil admits he cannot hear it without weeping tiny sick tears of nostalgia). If you see a vinyl copy of *Permanent Damage*, make sure the deluxe booklet of photos and lyrics is included. Released at the same time was bassist Jeff Simmons' collaboration with guitarist Craig Tarwater, *Lucille Has Messed My Mind Up*. Zappa 'salvaged' the album, donating the title-song and producing: a fine collection of power-driven, jazzy psychedelia. Other releases on Straight included spoken word by Lord Buckley (*A Most Immaculately Hip Aristocrat*) and Lenny Bruce (*The Berkeley Concert*); medieval folk-rock by Judy Henske and Jerry Yester (*Farewell Aldebaran*); shock rock by Alice Cooper (*Easy Action*); modal folk extensions by Tim Buckley (*Blue Afternoon*); and Sub-

Dylanology by Tim Dawe (*Penrod*). All these acts could be heard, along with 'Holiday In Berlin' and 'Willie The Pimp' by the Mothers, on *Zappèd*, a budget sampler issued by Warner Brothers.

When Zappa formed DiscReet Records, he put out albums by Ted Nugent & the Amboy Dukes (*Call Of The Wild*; *Tooth, Fang & Claw*) and Kathy Dalton (*Boogie Bands & One Night Stands*), but even the presence of Little Feat on the latter failed to make it anything extraordinary. Other production duties included Grand Funk Railroad's *Good Singin' Good Playin'* for EMI in 1976, to which Zappa contributed a guitar solo (something he regretted, as reviewers tended to use his solo to damn the playing on the rest of the record, and he liked Grand Funk a great deal), and violinist L. Shankar's *Touch Me There* for Zappa Records. Zappa and Ike Willis guested on the latter for Zappa's 'Dead Girls Of London', singing jointly under the name Stucco Homes. Zappa performed under another alias – Obdewl'l X – on two tracks of George Duke's *Feel* for MPS in 1974. Still harder to find is the CD by Prazsky Vyber named *Adieu CA* [AP 0001-2311], with Zappa playing guitar at Michael Kocab's concert to celebrate the evacuation of Russian troops from Prague on 24 June 1991 (Zappa only plays on one number, 'Blaznivy Reggae', and was mortified, because he hadn't touched the guitar in years).

Perhaps the most sublimely insane 'guest appearance' by Zappa is his version of John's Cage's 'silent' composition 4'33", contributed to *A Chance Operation: The John Cage Tribute* [Koch 3-7238] curated for Koch International Classics by Gary Davis in 1993, with booklet essays by David Revill and Richard Kostelanetz. Strangely enough, the track is great: you can actually hear Frank 'keep silent'!

Zappa has been bootlegged throughout his career, a practice he detested. In July 1991, Zappa licensed Rhino Records to 'bootleg his bootleggers', and release a boxed set of reproductions of his eight most famous ones.

Sound was slightly tweezed, but was derived from whatever the bootleggers had issued, often of fairly dubious quality (Zappa did not burrow into his archive and find his mixing-desk masters for these items; indeed, the whole project was handled by Rhino). The first *Beat The Boots* set was on both vinyl and CD: *As An Am Zappa* (31-Oct-'81), *The Ark: Mothers Of Invention* (Jul-'68), *Freaks & Motherfu*%!!@#* (11-May-'70), *Unmitigated Audacity* (12-May-'74), *Anyway The Wind Blows* (24-Feb-'79), *'Tis The Season To Be Jelly* (30-Sep-'67), *Saarbrucken 1979* (3-Sep-'78) and *Piquantique* (21-Aug-'73). The box included a cartoon representation of the *Overnite Sensation* Mothers in concert: the band were portrayed on the inside lid, with a 'pop-up' audience including Rhino Records' logo-rhino gleefully snipping the mic lead of a sleazy bootlegger. Fans bought these 'burnished turds' (as Zappa called them), so a second box was issued in 1992: *Disconnected Synapses* ('70), *Tengo Na Minchia Tanta* (Jun-'71), *Electric Aunt Jemima* ('68), *At The Circus* ('78/'70), *Swiss Cheese/Fire!* (12-Apr-'71), *Our Man In Nirvana* (8-Nov-'68), *Conceptual Continuity* (19-Nov-'77). Box two came with a 'beat the boots' beret and enamel badge, plus a lavish booklet assembled by Cal Schenkel. This wasn't quite the one he'd designed for *The Collected History & Improvisations Of The Mothers Of Invention* (a sneak preview of this was issued by in the mid-70s by Babylon Books, and it included Edgard Varèse's 1957 letter to Frank – the one now framed and hanging in his basement listening room – and a letter of rejection from Milt Rogers at Dot Records, the one about Zappa's music lacking 'commercial potential'), but still includes much fascinating material. Some record shops broke up the sets, so these 'bootleg bootlegs' may be found separately. In the fanzine *Society Pages*, Zappa recommended pursuit of extra listening material by swapping live tapes (as long as no money changes hands, this is not illegal). Anyone wishing to do this should begin by placing or answering a small-ad in the Zappa fanzine *T'Mershi Duween* (PO Box 86, Sheffield, S11 8XN, England).

Once Zappa had regained his master tapes from PolyGram and Warner Brothers, he reissued them in sets called *The Old Masters*. The boxes were silver, and each sported a different still life by Donald Roller Wilson. Inside were reproductions of the original albums, with gatefold sleeves and identical graphics (except that original record-label trademarks were replaced with the Barking Pumpkin logo). *The Old Masters* Box One was issued on 19 April 1985 and contained seven vinyl records: *Freak Out!* (a double), *Absolutely Free*, *Lumpy Gravy*, *We're Only In It For The Money*, *Cruising With Ruben And The Jets* and a *Mystery Disc* with such marvels as Captain Beefheart singing 'Metal Man Has Won His Wings' at Studio Z in Cucamonga, an early attempt at rock opera called 'I Was A Teenage Malt Shop', an acoustic-guitar 'Bossa Nova Pervertamento', the sped-up 'Speed-Freak Boogie' (which Mike Keneally insists is not 'sped-up', but a slowed-down recording played back at normal speed – welcome to the hardcore twiglet zone...) and an extract from the 'Uncle Frankie Show' where Zappa showed radio listeners how to play the backing to 'oh, a total of fifteen-thousand rock'n'roll songs' ('Run Home Slow Theme' and 'Charva' were later included on *Lost Episodes*; 'Why Don't You Do Me Right' and 'Big Leg Emma' on the Rykodisc issue of *Absolutely Free*). *The Old Masters* Box Two was released on 25 November 1986 and included *Uncle Meat* (a double), *Hot Rats*, *Burnt Weeny Sandwich*, *Weasels Ripped My Flesh*, *Chunga's Revenge*, *Fillmore East June 1970*, *Just Another Band From L.A.*. The booklet from *Uncle Meat* came housed in a black card sleeve sporting yet another spooky still life by Donald Roller Wilson, plus a reprint of Zappa's Conceptual Continuity Manifesto – an extraordinary piece of Philip K. Dick-like paranoid invention – from *Circular*, 'a weekly news device from Warner/Reprise', 20

September 1971. There was also another *Mystery Disc* with 22 minutes of the Mothers Of Invention at the Festival Hall in 1968, a studio recording of the anti-CIA 'Agency Man', and other scraps, including the original story of 'Willie The Pimp'. 'Wedding Dress Song'/'Handsome Cabin Boy' later appeared on *Lost Episodes. The Old Masters* Box Three appeared on 30 December 1987 and comprised: *Hot Rats: Waka/Jawaka*, *The Grand Wazoo*, *Over-Nite Sensation*, *Apostrophe (')*, *Roxy And Elsewhere* (a double), *One Size Fits All*, *Bongo Fury* and *Zoot Allures*. There was no *Mystery Disc* in Box Three: perhaps Zappa was already thinking that it would require the CD format to issue all the material he had hoarded on tape.

Zappa fans are famously demented, so it's safe to say that anything with 'Zappa' on it is wanted somewhere by someone (even books like this!). Now he's dead, the idea of 'official' Zappa product becomes increasingly tenuous, but not through lack of efforts by the extremely vigilant Zappa Family Trust. Rykodisc keeps interest in Zappa alive by issuing various collations of their own devise. *Strictly Commercial* was a brave attempt to select 'representative' tracks that probably pleased no-one except its compiler; *Strictly Genteel* was a 'classical' introduction that compiled Zappa's orchestral music. *Kill Ugly Radio, The Return Of The Son Of Kill Ugly Radio* and *Ditties And Beer* were brave attempts to interest radio-programmers in songs that were bound to land them in trouble. I've seen *Frank Zappa: Clean American Version*, a promotion-only CD, on offer at an inflated price, but it's hard to see who's buying, as all the material is available elsewhere. *Apostrophe(')* and *One Size Fits All* exist as 'Au20' audiophile releases on 24k gold CDs, while this very volume will be published by Omnibus in the year 2013 on rose-scented wrist-array chiffon, bound in pink-dyed, angora poodle-skin with goldleaf-tooling (provided enough hardcores show an interest...).

BIBLIOGRAPHY

Pamela Des Barres, *I'm With The Band: Confessions Of A Groupie*
(NY: Jove, 1988).

Miss Pamela of the GTO's gives an insider's view of freakdom in Los Angeles; hilarious and poignant.

Michael Gray, Mother! *The Frank Zappa Story* (1985; London:
Plexus, 1993).

Contains some refreshing observations from Pamela Zarubica (the first Suzy Creamcheese); the last half is flawed by Gray's pompous 'sexual politics'.

James Joyce, *Finnegans Wake*
(London: Faber, 1949).

The only 'book' quite as good as a Zappa record, and stuffed with conceptual continuity.

Franz Kafka, 'In The Penal Colony' (1919) *Metamorphosis And Other Stories*
(London: Penguin, 1961).

If you're going to supplement listening to Zappa with literature, this is the one: the blueprint for the monstrosity that is *We're Only In It For The Money*. Terrifying.

Richard Kostelanetz, *The Frank Zappa Companion: Four Decades Of Commentary*

(NY: Schirmer, 1997).

Notable for the reprint of an article in *Contemporary Music Review* by a certain Ben Watson which claimed that Zappa's concept was in advance of both Cage and Boulez (a thesis which has produced remarkably little response from academia); also some early situationist/collage work by Out To Lunch, and a note from Vaclav Havel.

Nigey Lennon, *Being Frank: My Time With Frank Zappa*

(LA: California Classics, 1995).

Written by a guitarist and arranger who toured with The Mothers, this has an unusual amount of musical perception. A moving account.

Karl Marx, *Capital*

(London: 1867).

The other book that's as good as a Zappa record.

Barry Miles Frank Zappa: A Visual Documentary

(London: Omnibus, 1993).

Lists all the data off the back of the Rykodisc albums, so a slightly pointless purchase for the completist, but does contain some apposite quotes and photos, and a useful date-by-date gig list.

Neil Slaven, *Zappa: Electric Don Quixote*

(London: Omnibus, 1996).

A scissors-and-paste biography drawing from most of the journalistic sources, but with remarkable paucity of blinding insight. Distinctly unZappaesque.

David Walley, *No Commercial Potential: The Saga Of Frank Zappa*

(1972; updated edition, New York: Da Capo, 1996).

The first biography, one that started out as 'official' before everything went predictably pumpkin-shaped. The account of early Zappa is essential, but Walley's later judgments are skewed by the author's lack of engagement and ludicrous self-importance.

Ben Watson, *Frank Zappa: The Negative Dialectics Of Poodle Play*

(1994; fourth edition with amendments and postfix, London: Quartet, 1996).

My humble attempt to put Zappa up there in the pantheon alongside Heraclitus, Shakespeare and Kenny Process Team. Ignored by academics, reviled by journalists – and imaginatively-challenged 'hardcores'.

Frank Zappa, *Them Or Us (The Book)*

(LA: Barking Pumpkin, 1984).

Zappa's own 351-page, film-treatment style 're-mix' of themes from 'Billy the Mountain', Hunchentoot, *Joe's Garage*, *Francesco Zappa* and *Thing-Fish*, in mid-'80s-style continuous-feed-stationery computer print-out. Essential for all conceptual-continuity freaks and 'not for intellectuals or other dead people'. Wild.

Frank Zappa with Peter Occhiogrosso, *The Real Frank Zappa Book*

(NY: Poseidon, 1989).

Zappa's account of the early years, plus opinions on music and politics. Trenchant, but not as brilliant as the records.